BLACK BRITIS HISTORY

SELECTED STUDIES

Northamptonshire
Black History Association

First published: 2010
Published by Northamptonshire Black History Association
Copyright (C) Northamptonshire Black History Association 2010

ISBN: 978-0-9557139-7-2

Northamptonshire Black History Association
Doddridge Centre
109 St James Road
Northampton NN5 5LD
Tel: 01604 590967   Email: admin@northants-black-history.org.uk
Website: www.northants-black-history.org.uk

Printed by Eagle Graphics (Printers) Ltd
Unit 1, Firbank Court
Leighton Buzzard LU7 4YJ
Tel: 01525 384893   Email: graphics@egp.uk.com

Other recent NBHA publications:

Children's Story Book (2007)
*The Story of Walter Tull: Professional Black Footballer
and First Black Officer in the British Army*

Illustrated History Book (2008)
Sharing the Past: Northamptonshire Black History (2008)

Teaching Packs (2007-08):
*Walter Tull: Sport, War and Challenging Adversity (KS 1, KS 2/3, KS 3)
Representations of Empire (KS 2/3)
Living Memories (KS 2/3)*
(NBHA publications available from NBHA and through www.Amazon.co.uk)

On-Line Resources (2008-09):
*From Slavery to Emancipation
Northamptonshire in Global Context*
(available free of charge on NBHA website)

CONTENTS

అఇఆ

Chapter	Page
1. Introduction	1
2. Amongst the Aristocracy and Underclass: The Lives of Black People and Attitudes to Race in Eighteenth Century Britain *by Anne-Marie Sandos*	3
3. Bristol and the Slave Trade *by Harriet Smith*	14
4. Henry Sylvester Williams: His Achievements and Influence *by Maxim Ferreira*	27
5. Claudia Jones *by Elnora Latchman*	38
6. Unsung Black British Heroes of the Second World War *by Pauline Clarke*	47
7. West Indian Soldiers in World War II *by Hugh Smith*	58
8. Encounters with Bob Marley and his Reggae Music *by June White-Gulley*	68
9. Rastafarianism in Jamaica and Britain *by Alecia Kowalska*	80
10. Caribbean Food from Past to Present *by Shirley Brownbill*	91
11. Sake Dean Mahomed *by Heather Knighton*	100
12. Foreign Shores: A Brief History of Lascars in Britain *by Joseph Bench*	109
13. Sophia Duleep Singh - Princess and Activist *by Jean Bouch*	118
14. Islamophobia: Historical Stereotypes and Changing Attitudes towards Muslims in Britain *by Babul Miah*	130

Chapter 1

Introduction

This collection of essays is a reflection of ongoing efforts to introduce Black British history to students, as well as adding to collective consciousness of British history in both a local and national context.

The essays encompass a wide variety of topics and eras. They range over the past three hundred years, providing nine studies which link Britain to Africa, North America and the Caribbean followed by four studies connected with the Indian sub-continent. What is implicit in the writing, and has been explicitly mentioned by many of the writers during their research, is that the history you will be reading about here was almost universally ignored or unknown in 'traditional' British education, especially as it existed and exists in the National Curriculum.

The book was written by University of Northampton students who took part in an evening course titled Special Studies in Black British History between 2006-09. This course is in itself an effort to include Black British people into 'accepted' British historical frameworks. It is the outcome of a fruitful partnership between the University and Northamptonshire Black History Association, a community-based membership organisation established in 2005. Northamptonshire Black History Association grew from the legacies of a successful lottery-funded research project. It is now an educational charity dedicated to increasing knowledge and understanding of Black British history both in Northamptonshire and further afield. Its activities include publication of educational books and other resources, as well as a programme of community history events and ongoing work to develop and safeguard the record of Black British history.

The University of Northampton is one of only three British universities currently providing students with courses in Black British history. One of the main innovative elements of these evening courses is that any member of the community can become a student: participation in the courses is not limited to University undergraduates. Many of the most interesting and original essays were written by mature students and those who had not been in formal education for many years prior to taking the course. Having relevant life experiences has provided them with an added desire to learn what was virtually ignored in their compulsory education.

Reading these essays will give readers an understanding of various aspects of the diverse history of Black people in Britain. As one of the writers said, "with Black history being omitted (from the school curriculum in England), I was starved for it and now I'm lavishing in it."You are invited to lavish in the diverse and interesting history within this book.

Northamptonshire Black History Association wishes to thank the University of Northampton for its valuable support, including sponsorship of the present book. Authors of the Selected Studies would also like to thank families and friends for their encouragement, which helped to make the book possible (you all know who you are). Whilst the University has helped to meet the printer's bill, authors and editors have put in many hours of unpaid labour. Thanks are due to the editorial team: Anne-Marie Sandos, Monica Babb, Jean Bouch, Julia Bush, Maxim Ferreira, Ruchira Pounds, George Watley and June White-Gulley. Ultimately the book rests upon the commitment and talents of its authors: Joseph Bench, Jean Bouch, Shirley Brownbill, Pauline Clarke, Maxim Ferreira, Heather Knighton, Alecia Kowalska, Elnora Latchman, Babul Miah, Anne-Marie Sandos, Harriet Smith, Hugh Smith and June White-Gulley. We hope that you will enjoy their work.

Northamptonshire Black History Association, June 2010

Note: Authors and editors have made efforts to acknowledge the primary and secondary research sources used in the writing of this book. Please contact Northamptonshire Black History Association if you wish to suggest any corrections, and these will be made as soon as possible. The views and opinions expressed in these studies are those of the individual authors and do not necessarily reflect those of Northamptonshire Black History Association.

Chapter 2

Amongst the Aristocracy and Underclass: The Lives of Black People and Attitudes to Race in Eighteenth Century Britain

by Anne-Marie Sandos

This chapter explores the lives of Black people in the eighteenth century and how attitudes towards race shaped the conditions in which they existed. Trade links meant that the majority of Blacks were employed as servants or slaves to the upper classes or were concentrated in urban slums trying to make a living for themselves amongst the poorest of the poor. Life on two opposite ends of the spectrum meant that the circumstances in which Black people lived were marked either by comfortable servitude or excluded poverty. Black people, whether treasured pet or destitute vagabond, were unified by a struggle for self-actualisation and rights; living within a society which they were prevented from being part of. These seemingly disparate lifestyles were shaped by a set of common attitudes within Britain during the eighteenth century.

For the purpose of this chapter the term Black relates to people of African descent, either directly from Africa or the colonies. After setting the historical context the study explores the lives of Black people who lived amongst the aristocracy. The next section examines evidence relating to Black people amongst the underclass. Then the chapter explores eighteenth century attitudes to race and how these shaped the experiences of Black people at the time.

Historical Context

Prior to the eighteenth century it was common for Black people to be brought to England as servants and slaves to the upper classes. So much so that in 1596 Queen Elizabeth I issued an edict demanding they leave. This move proved unpopular and was either blocked or evaded by their masters or employers. There are records of Black artists performing in Britain from the sixteenth century. King James I even had Black servants for a range of roles, including fashion accessories and minstrels.[2]

In the eighteenth century most Black people arrived in England either directly or indirectly as a result of the Triangular Trade which saw the exchange of goods between England, the Caribbean and Africa. Amongst these goods were tea, cotton, sugar, arms and people. From the mid eighteenth century the Abolition movement gathered pace and support. A court case concerning a slave called Somerset gave impetus to the cause. Somerset was brought to Britain from America. During his time in Britain he ran away. Although slavery was legal in the colonies it was not recognised on the mainland. He was recaptured, brutally beaten, clapped in irons and put on a slave ship. Amongst the claims and counter claims Somerset was accused of duping his master by absenting himself from service, resulting in him being effectively put on bail for the course of the trial despite him being the plaintiff. The case judge Mansfield ruled that he could not be forcibly removed from Britain against his will but also insisted that the ruling was specific to the case and he was set free. During this century court rulings around slavery were contradictory, highlighting the ambiguous status of Black people in the society. The Black community and abolitionists saw this ruling as a step towards freedom, whilst for slavers the ruling threatened to bring chaos creating a risk to their control in the plantations.[3]

Evidence held by the National Archives shows "Black people were an integral part of 18th century Britain; they worked in a wide variety of occupations, reacted to atrocities, campaigned to end slavery, became politically active and had a lively social life."[4] The National Archives contain evidence of established social networks and communities of Black people. "Black servants and settlers in London developed into a genuine community. Black servants and slaves gravitated towards each other's company, meeting in homes of their masters, in their favourite local tavern, celebrating together and most crucially passing on news and information."[5]

Amongst the Aristocracy: Black Servants and Slaves

Black servants and slaves to the upper classes were status symbols. Having a Black servant showed that you were moneyed, cultured and cosmopolitan.

century."[15] They became so much a part of the social landscape that the artist William Hogarth included them in engravings satirizing social conditions. They found themselves in settlements of squalid, run down, back to back slums. Their areas were notoriously dangerous and crime was rife, from pick-pocketing to murder.[16]

In 1783 Black immigrants from North America who fought for Britain in the American war now arrived to claim their promised freedom. "The British had periodically used slaves in the fighting and as support labourers (often linked to the promise of freedom). When the defeated British finally quit [the United States], they escaped north to Canada or back to Britain with those former slaves who had sided with them in the war."[17] However, strict rules regarding trades aimed at preventing migration made it impossible to gain steady employment.

In 1731 immigrants to London were forbidden by the Lord Mayor's proclamation to learn trades.[18] This law effectively banished Black people to begging or stealing. Ramdin argues,"The Black poor were among the poorest of the poor in London."[19] Conspicuous by their skin colour, their situation was precarious as they faced daily dilemmas. "On the one hand, hunger and poverty forced them to beg and steal, while on the other they were faced with the possibility of deportation and slavery."[20] British legal institutions were not sympathetic to the plight of these soldiers. "Commissioners dealing with claims for compensation for losses in that fighting looked much less favourably on Black claims…[they] felt that it was sufficient that the supplicant Blacks secured their freedom."[21]

Communities developed networks"that could be mobilized for the purpose of social and political action."[22] They offered each other support in difficult times:"When in 1773, for example, two Black men were confined to Bridewell prison for begging more than 300 black people not only visited them but provided for their economic support."[23] Whilst some Londoners offered their support others were concerned about the strain it put on the community. As Black people were not eligible for poor law support the burden fell upon the parish council and the good will of neighbours who were also in straitened circumstances.

In 1786 a committee was formed to provide relief for London's Black poor and within months more than four hundred had been provided with food, clothing and lodging.[24] Famous Black abolitionist writer and campaigner

Olaudah Equiano was involved with a plan to send London's Black poor to Sierra Leone. The plan proved a disaster, beset with problems of recruitment and administration, and the majority of those that went to settle died within a year. The consequences of the plan were tragic and highlight the desperate circumstances of the times.

Making a living from the street was necessary for those surviving amongst the underclass. There were a number of Black street performers and buskers who entertained the public. One such performer became a well-known character, gaining notoriety. Billy Waters was believed to have been a soldier in the American War of Independence. He worked as a fiddler and was commonly seen outside the Adelphi Theatre. He was famously caricatured by Cruickshank and had figurines made of him. Records from St Giles' workhouse showed that he became ill and spent his final days there, where he was elected king of the beggars.[25]

Life was hard for the working class in eighteenth century Britain and opportunities were limited for everyone.[26] An early Black writer gives a detailed description of poverty in England in the eighteenth century: "A Narrative of the most Remarkable Particulars in the Life of James Albert Ukasaw Gronniosaw, an African Prince, as Related by Himself." Gerzina notes that his writing describes not only the situation of the Black community but "gives us a picture of the formidability of life for the working poor. Food, housing, medical care, burial: those fundamentals were often inadequate, sometimes non-existent."[27] While Black people living amongst the underclass shared common experiences of poverty with the White community, they were experiencing additional hardships due to the mind-set of those in authority.

Attitudes to Race

Ideologies of racial stratification were created by intellectuals to justify and promote White economic interests and subordinate Black people in Britain and the colonies. "The pivotal figure in this development [of racial stratification] was the philosopher John Locke who played a large part in the creation of the Board of Trade, the architect of the old colonial system." He was a proponent of the idea that human beings can be ordered according to physical traits such as skin colour. At the time there was a 'cult of physiognomy' which held that you could read morality into how people looked. The ideas of goodness, beauty and truth became linked and the definition of beauty was based on European ideals.[29]

These attitudes were disseminated by the social elite and used as a means of social control:"for about 300 years racism has had a precise social function. It has functioned as an ideology: a system of false ideas justifying the exploitation of and domination of people."[30] Ramdin argues that"plantocracy racism supported by British capitalists, politicians, historians and influential people of letters, engendered a dogmatic belief in white supremacy and institutionalised racism in Britain and her colonial possessions."[31]

The eighteenth century was an age of money made through the slave trade. Thousands of Black slaves were brought to Britain by merchants and planters. People believed"the whole earth is the market of Britain."[32] Slavery was rationalised on economic grounds as necessary, making morality a secondary consideration. The moral justification was that it was benevolent as the trade provided jobs for poor Whites and saved Blacks from tyranny.[33]

These attitudes meant that the status of Black people was subordinate to White people, whether amongst the aristocracy or the underclass, as social attitudes of the decision-makers and society in general sought to justify their position within a social and economic framework. This situation led to "thousands of Black people living and working under a legal system which recognised most of them only as property and denied the most fundamental rights."[34] These attitudes were enshrined in law and institutional racism. However the relationship was not straightforward: "The presence of black slaves in Britain introduced a new social problem. The ownership of human beings as property was a challenge to common law."[35]

In order to resolve and rationalise inconsistencies, ideological and psychological justifications were developed to legitimise the position of Black people. Gerzina argues: "This growing presence [of Black people] challenged English sensibilities about race and fairness and xenophobia…to deal with this contradiction a whole intellectual industry of justifying slavery was necessary, finding exhaustive expression in David Hume's assertion of Negro inferiority in Bryan Edwards' and Edward Long's treatise on the West Indies and running through Carlyle's infamous Discourse on the Nigger Question."[36]

Although the rise of abolitionism in the mid-eighteenth century marked a challenge to institutional attitudes to Black people, even progressives stopped short of expounding equality. Writer Sir John Fielding, in his extracts from period laws, worried in 1765 that Black people were being inappropriately influenced by notions of equality once they got to Britain.[37]

Abolitionism had become fashionable, a *cause-celebre* with artists, writers, clergy and the working classes rallying to the cause. Dabydeen argues that by 1770 England was deluged with anti-slavery verse.[38] Wordsworth, Blake, Southey and Cowper added to the artistic genre. He is cynical about the White writers' motives: "Unlike the Black writers of the 18th century whose finances and very lives were bound up with their literary productions, English writers merely exploited the slave theme for their own gain and recognition."[39]

Towards the end of the century the idea of Black inferiority was challenged. Sancho's letters were cited by the abolitionist movement as an "outstanding refutation of the idea that Black people lacked souls, intellects or rational facilities."[40] In 1789, William Dickson's *Letters on Slavery* argued that poor standards of education and morality were actually perpetuated by plantation life.[41] This argument was beginning to become adopted by more people as Black and White people developed closer relationships.

Parish records show numerous mixed marriages across the country. The National Archives have records from 1731 showing Englishman Warren Hull married Maria Sambo in Earls Colne.[42] Mixed marriages were generally accepted within the community as they tended to happen amongst the lower classes: "However concerns were raised in the press about their impact on the country. In 1773, one outraged correspondent wrote to the *London Chronicle* begging the public to 'save the natural beauty of Britons from contamination'."[43] A writer and social commentator of the time raged, "in almost every village, are to be seen a little race of mullattoes, mischievous as monkeys and infinitely more dangerous."[44]

Over the course of the eighteenth century English racial attitudes can be seen evolving from a kind of naïve and not necessarily benign curiosity into surprisingly modern and complicated beliefs about race.[45] Sentimentality and hypocrisy surrounded attitudes towards Black people. The eighteenth century elite found it easier to connect emotionally with poetry and plays about the plight of slaves than through everyday contact: "A slave sold in a coffee house in Liverpool or run off from a master in Bristol, or parodied with a padlocked collar in London, ironically aroused far less public sympathy than a White man or women pretending to be a Black person in the theatre."[46] Black people were separated from the rest of British society, working within a class system but rarely finding a place within it. The majority of Blacks found themselves dependent on the goodwill and humanity of their White employers, masters or patrons. Racial attitudes were created by those of the elite who stood to gain from the slave trade. The system depended on the dehumanisation of Black people; however growing contact with Black people themselves challenged these attitudes.

1 G. Gerzina, *Black England: Life Before Emancipation* (London: John Murray, 1995), p. 4.

2 Gerzina, p. 4.

3 Gerzina, pp. 116-132.

4 National Archives, 'Black Presence: Asian and Black History in Britain 1500-1850/ Work and Community'. Available from: **http://www.nationalarchives.gov.uk/ pathways/blackhsitory/work_community/ docs** (accessed 15 April 2008).

5 J. Walvin, 'The Man and His Times', in C. Phillips (ed.), *Ignatius Sancho: An African Man of Letters* (London: National Portrait Gallery Publications, 1997), p. 99.

6 Gerzina, p. 16.

7 Gerzina, p. 15.

8 R. Ramdin, *The Making of the Black Working Class in Britain* (Aldershot: Wildwood House,1987), p. 7.

9 Gerzina, p. 39.

10 R. King, 'Ignatius Sancho and Portraits of the Black Elite', in Phillips, p. 16.

11 S. Sandhu, 'An African Man of Letters', in Phillips, p. 59.

12 Sandhu, pp. 62-63.

13 'The Black 18th Century', BBC 4, 3 July 2006.

14 Gerzina, p. 19.

15 J. Walvin, 'The Man and His Times', in Phillips, p. 108.

16 National Archives, 'Black Presence', **www.nationalarchives.gov.uk/pathwys/ blackhistory/work_community/docs** (accessed 15 April 2008).

17 Walvin, p. 107.

18 Gerzina, pp. 18-19.

19 Ramdin, p. 16.

20 Ramdin, p. 17.

21 Walvin, pp. 107-8.

22 Gerzina, p. 24.

23 Gerzina, p.6.

24 Walvin, p. 108.

25 National Archives, 'Black Presence', **www.nationalarchives.gov.uk/pathways/ blackhistory/culture/music.htm** (accessed 15 April 2008).

26 National Archives, 'Black Presence', **www.nationalarchives.gov.uk/pathways/ blackhistory/work_community/docs** (accessed 15 April 2008).

27 Gerzina, pp 21-22.

28 P. Fryer, *Black People in the British Empire, An Introduction* (London: Pluto Press, 1989) , p. 65.

29 'The Black 18th Century', BBC4.

30 Fryer, p. 61.

31 Ramdin, p. 7.

32 D. Dabydeen, *The Black Presence in English Literature* (Manchester: Manchester University Press, 1985), p. 26.

33 Dabydeen, p. 28.

34 Gerzina, p. 2.

35 Ramdin, p. 9.

36 Gerzina, p. 6.

37 Gerzina, p. 24.

38 Dabydeen, p. 44.

39 Dabydeen, p. 45.

40 Sandhu, p. 67.

41 Ramdin, p. 15.

42 National Archives, 'Black Presence', **www.nationalarchives.gov.uk/pathways/ blackhistory/work_community/docs** (accessed 15 April 2008).

43 National Archives, 'Black Presence', (accessed 15 April 2008).

44 Gerzina, p. 22.

45 Gerzina, p. 25.

46 Gerzina, p. 7.

Bibliography

Dabydeen, D., *The Black Presence in English Literature* (Manchester: Manchester University Press, 1985)

Fryer, P., *Staying Power: the History of Black People in Britain* (London: Pluto Press, 1984)

Fryer, P., *Black People in the British Empire. An Introduction* (London: Pluto Press, 1989)

Gerzina, G., *Black England: Life Before Emancipation* (London: John Murray 1995)

King, R., *'Ignatius Sancho and Portraits of the Black Elite'* in Caryl Phillips (ed.), *Ignatius Sancho: African Man of Letters* (London: National Portrait Gallery Publications,1997)

Ramdin, R., *The Making of the Black Working Class in Britain* (Aldershot: Wildwood House, 1987)

Sandhu, S., *'An African Man of Letters'* in Caryl Phillips (ed.), Ignatius Sancho: An African Man of Letters (London: National Portrait Gallery Publications, 1997)

Walvin, J., *'The Man and His Times'* in Caryl Phillips (ed.), *Ignatius Sancho: An African Man of Letters* (London: National Portrait Gallery Publications, 1997)

BBC 4, 'The Black 18th Century', 3 July 2006

National Archives ,'Black Presence: Asian and Black History in Britain 1500-1850/ Culture', **www.nationalarchives.gov.uk/pathways/blackhistory/culture/music.htm** (accessed 15 April 2008)

National Archives ,'Black Presence: Asian and Black History in Britain 1500-1850 /Work and Community', **www.nationalarchives.gov.uk/pathways/blackhistory/work_community/docs** (accessed 15 April 2008)

Chapter 3

Bristol and the Slave Trade

by Harriet Smith

This chapter is about the slave trade in the city of Bristol. England may have been late in comparison with other European colonial powers to fully exploit the slave trade, but it was a leading trader by 1676. Britain continued to be so until 1807, when it became one of the first major European countries to abolish the slave trade. Cities such as London, Liverpool and Bristol played a central role in the transatlantic trade in slaves, primarily because of their ports.[1] This study covers the background to slavery in Bristol, its economic importance to the city, Bristol's involvement in the abolition movement, and the legacy left behind by the slave trade in Bristol. Research sources include literature found at Bristol Central Library, websites and a visit to the British Empire and Commonwealth Museum in Bristol, and in particular to the exhibition on slavery called 'Breaking the Chains'.

Bristol and African Trade

From the late fourteenth to the mid-eighteenth century, Bristol was a significant British port and brought considerable income and wealth to its people through a number of seaborne trading routes. Bristol ship owners were constantly looking for new ways to make money. Financiers from London and Bristol put money towards the initial exploratory voyages.[2] This desire for wealth often overshadowed moral concerns about the type of trade in which they engaged. In the early twelfth century, for example, Bristol's merchants were heavily involved in transporting child slaves to Ireland. Not surprisingly, therefore, as the West African slave trade began to develop local merchants lobbied King William III to permit them the opportunity to take part in what was, by then, a monopoly granted by royal charter to the Royal African Company. This company was a crown institution which also involved some London merchants. Subsequently the slave trade became a major economic force in Bristol, leading to much prosperity through buildings and investments extending as far as the nearby city of Bath.

The West African slave trade provided Bristol with many economic opportunities, despite not always being the prime transporter of slaves. Compared to Liverpool or London, Bristol may not on the face of it appear to have seen quite the same through-put, but according to Madge Dresser recent figures show that between 1698 and 1807 there were 2008 slaving voyages leaving Bristol which in turn transported some 486,000 slaves to the New World.[3] Over a similar period Liverpool delivered well over twice that sum, yet author David Richardson reminds us that Bristol nevertheless played a crucial role in the trade's early development: "Bristol merchants responded with greater alacrity than their rivals in other out ports to the opportunities offered by the Act of 1668 and... in general it was Bristol merchants more than those of either London or Liverpool that provided most of the impetus behind the substantial expansion of British trade with Africa that occurred between 1713 and 1730."[4]

Whilst it may be true that Bristol did not deal with as many slaves as its counterparts in London and Liverpool, it was nevertheless the nation's number one slaving port from around 1723 to around 1743. By the mid-1740s, when the city's role as a slaving port was overtaken by Liverpool, Bristol had already helped to establish an effective trading and political infrastructure to support the trade. Furthermore, and by his own admission, Richardson may well have underestimated the number of slaves moving through Bristol as his survey did not take account of all the Bristol ships operating in Africa.[5]

Bristol's growth, as a result, was not confined merely to the economic. Its population grew significantly as well. In 1700 it had around 20,000 citizens, but only 100 years later this figure had tripled. The slave trade provided employment for all kinds of crafts and tradesmen. Not only were goods manufactured for trading in Africa but ships had to be built, repaired and fitted out. Finance and insurance, as well as supplies, had to be arranged for each voyage. Its growth as a slaving port also brought unwelcome notoriety. Runaways, criminals, adventures and the gullible all flocked to Bristol in search of a better life.[6]

Bristol and the West Indies

The economic boom of the eighteenth century in Bristol was fuelled by more than just the trade and transportation of African slaves to the Caribbean colonies. Many valuable goods were brought back from the Caribbean which fed the city's developing industries. Rum distilleries, chocolate producers, coffee houses, cotton merchants and tobacconists all prospered from the West Indian trade. However, the sugar production industry in Bristol saw the greatest growth during this period. It was second only to London for importing sugar which was processed in the city's refineries. By the 1750s Bristol had over one sixth of all refineries in Britain. Overall, by the end of the 18th century around 40 per cent of Bristol's income came from, or related to, slavery.

The transatlantic slave trade needed men and women with a range of skills to service the industry and newly arrived aspirant workers found jobs on Bristol's docks as labourers involved in the building, equipping and repairing of vessels. By the eighteenth century, Bristol had eclipsed its rivals and was responsible for half the ships leaving Britain. Its involvement in the slave trade had a considerable effect on the city, transforming it into one of Britain's foremost cities with a thriving social and intellectual life.

The main beneficiaries of Bristol's economic growth from slave labour were the members of the local merchant classes. They set up the Society of Merchant Venturers, a group still in existence today, which was heavily involved in the infamous triangular trade whereby manufactured goods were shipped to West Africa and traded for slaves who in turn were transported to the West Indies and exchanged for sugar, rum and molasses which was brought back to Britain.[7] In Bristol itself, the Merchants also immersed themselves in local politics. Their power in the city grew immeasurably. Sixteen of their members who were also slave traders and ship-owners served as Masters of the Society, sixteen served as Sheriff of Bristol, ten as aldermen and eleven as Mayor. Involvement in the trade was common amongst many of the city's leading families. Later, however, some of their members were among the first voices to condemn slavery and call for its abolition.[8]

Abolition and Bristol's involvement

Although Bristol was heavily involved in the slave trade in the sixteenth century, there were occasional local protests against it. Minor campaigns were formed with women playing a prominent role. These campaigns were often referred to as the abolition movement and aimed to inform people of the horrors of slavery and to persuade both the public and Members of Parliament that it should be made illegal. It was not, however, until the mid eighteenth century that opposition to the slave trade became a major issue.

At national level, the real campaign for the abolition of the slave trade did not get under way until the 1780s. It was led in Parliament by William Wilberforce and supported at the grass-roots level by a combination of Quakers, evangelical Christians and other individuals committed to the principles of human rights including many Black people who had been enslaved. At first, progress was limited to the regulation of conditions aboard British slave ships. These were somewhat improved after 1788, following the Dolben Act. A year earlier, Wilberforce had introduced a Bill in Parliament to abolish the slave trade. Originally it was thrown out, but Wilberforce and others continued to fight. By 1792 the House of Commons had agreed to end the slave trade in another four years, but war with France broke out and saved the planters for a while at least. Wilberforce and his supporters continued to press Parliament to free all slaves within the British Empire. Planters and merchants fought this tooth and nail and a delegation from Bristol petitioned the British government to protect their interests.[9]

Despite the relentless doggedness of anti-slavery campaigners both inside and outside Parliament, abolition was not achieved until 1807. By this time, given the wars with post-revolutionary France, the political climate was hostile to further reform. Consequently the formal emancipation of those already enslaved in the British colonies would have to wait three more decades until 1833 and the Emancipation Act. Even then, true freedom did not come until 1838, when the apprenticeship system was abolished.[10]

Bristol responded to the abolition movement by becoming the first city outside London to set up a committee for the abolition of the slave trade. In 1788 Thomas Clarkson, a leading campaigner against the slave trade, visited Bristol to collect evidence.[11] Clarkson was a young clergyman who had studied at Cambridge, however the cause moved him to change direction and become an active campaigner.[12] He risked his personal safety to gather details about the slave trade, researching in the taverns of Bristol as he mixed with the sailors of slave ships. From such seamen he was able to gather strong evidence of the cruelty of slave raids and the horrors of the Middle Passage.[13] He collected many instruments of torture used on slave ships and exhibited this apparatus, which shocked people into actively supporting the abolitionists and forming committees.[14] One such committee was set up in Bristol. John Pinney and Richard Bright, two of Bristol's leading slave owners, were furious and attacked Clarkson in the local press.[15]

Clarkson found that, in general, Bristolians were against the slave trade. However, given the economic benefits it brought locally, most were reluctant to criticise it openly. The first public meeting in Bristol to discuss abolition was held on 28 January 1788 and resolved to establish a committee, to collect money for the cause and to start a petition. Many of its first members were Quakers with family slaving connections. The committee approached the government about the slave trade, held meetings and circulated petitions. The committee members ensured that the Bristol newspapers were full of poems and letters condemning the slave trade.[16]

Some eight hundred people volunteered to sign the first Bristol petition against the slave trade in 1799. This was one of the first political campaigns to see women taking an active role, especially in the boycott of slave- produced sugar. Women played a vital part in the campaign to abolish slavery, even thought at that time they did not have the right to vote. One woman, the Bristol poet Hannah More, wrote a poem specifically designed to back up the Wilberforce political campaign. Later, some women employed similar campaign techniques to those of the abolition quest during the struggle for female suffrage.[17] Before the poem was published More showed it to some members of Bristol's Baptist Academy which, it was said, infused a whole generation of missionaries with anti-slavery principles. Joseph Cottle would later go on to join the poet Robert Southey and his friend Samuel Taylor Coleridge in writing against the slave trade.[18]

Although the tide of public opinion in Bristol was beginning to turn against slavery, there were still many people locally with a powerful vested interest in its continuation. Much of Bristol's prosperity was tied up with the trade and the Merchant Venturers continued to support it. However, even amongst the Merchants there were some dissenting voices emerging. In the same year that Thomas Clarkson visited Bristol, Joseph Harford was the Master of the Society. He then became chairman of the first provincial committee to promote the abolition movement. A year later the Merchant Venturers' Society itself began campaigning against the slave trade.[19]

Somewhat ironically, Wilberforce died some four weeks before the Emancipation Act of 1838 became law and took effect from 1 August 1834. It marked the end of the plantation system. Many plantations soon collapsed as a result. Planters could not afford to play the new wages and Black people were reluctant to carry on working in the sugar fields and boiling houses. Many planters went bankrupt, in spite of the compensation they had received from the British government.[20]

Bristol's Legacy from Slavery

The remaining legacy of the slave trade in Bristol today, it can be argued, takes the form of architecture, including monuments and memorials, and can also be found within the minds of local people. The recent 200-year anniversary of the abolition of the British slave trade was strongly commemorated in Bristol and sparked considerable debate. Furthermore, it forms a part of the history now taught to Bristol school children.

English Heritage recently launched a website looking at the story of slavery, the abolition movement, and the lives of Black people between the seventeenth and nineteenth centuries. Bristol and the South West featured heavily on the website, which was also accompanied by a special leaflet called 'Sites of Memory – The Slave Trade and Abolition'[21] showing houses, docks, graves, plaques and memorials in and around the Bristol area.

One example is Pero's Bridge, built in 1999, which was named in honour of Pero Jones, a slave who lived in Bristol from around 1753 to 1798. He was the personal servant of John Pinney, a famous merchant and slave trader. Pero came to England in 1783. By 1793 he was the servant of the Pinney family in Bristol, in their house near the top of Park Street. It is argued that naming the new bridge Pero's Bridge was an important act by Bristol City Council for three reasons. The first reason is that it recognises the contribution of Black people to the development of the city. Secondly, it acknowledges that slavery contributed to Bristol's wealth. Thirdly, it shows that the city wants people to appreciate its regret for the suffering caused, and believes that the racism of the past should no longer be hidden.[22]

Pinney's legacy to the slave trade is further demonstrated by the continuing existence of the Georgian House Museum, just off Park Street. The Pinney family house was bought with inherited profits from their slave plantations on the island of Nevis and is exhibited as it might have looked in the eighteenth century, providing an insight into life above and below stairs. On 1 August 2007, Emancipation Day, a new interpretation of the Georgian House was launched as part of the bi-centennial commemoration. Visitors can learn about how the profits from slavery helped to shape the city of Bristol as we know it today.[23]

A special museum exhibition in Bristol was designed to commemorate its involvement in the slave trade. The 'Breaking the Chains' exhibition was housed at the British Empire and Commonwealth Museum. This million-pound Heritage Lottery Fund exhibition was created to mark the two hundredth anniversary of the 1807 Abolition Act. The entire top floor of the Museum was dedicated to telling the story of the transatlantic trade in enslaved people, and the means by which this brutal transportation was brought to an end.[24]

Another of Bristol's famous slave-related landmarks is the Colston Hall, which was named after Edward Colston. It is now a prominent venue for concert and art events. Colston made his fortune as a sugar merchant and member of the Royal African Company with interests in St Kitts, and was also famous for his charity and philanthropy in Bristol where he was born. He founded almshouses at St Michael's Hill and supported local schools. A statue of him was erected in Colston Avenue, Bristol, in the nineteenth century.[25]

Yet another important place in Bristol with slavery connections is Queen's Square, which was home to wealthy merchants with interests in the colonies. Henry Bright was mayor of Bristol and a prominent merchant of the slave trade. He lived at 29 Queen Street, which is now the regional headquarters of English Heritage.[26] Other places with slave trade connections include Blaise Castle, built by slave trade investor Thomas Farr. It was said that Farr could run to the top of the hill and see his ships sailing back up the river Avon from the castle.[27] In nearby Stroud there is a grand arch on Pagan Hill, built in 1834. It is one of the few remaining memorials and reputedly one of the oldest anti-slavery memorials in Britain.[28] There can also be found a plaque at the Seven Stars Pub in Thomas Lane, Redcliffe, Bristol which marks where the leading abolitionist Thomas Clarkson stayed in 1788, gathering evidence on the conditions aboard slave ships.[29]

The legacy of the slave trade in Bristol does not just reside in physical markers like buildings and follies. This was clearly demonstrated by the bicentennial commemoration of the Abolition Act and even today the subject sparks fierce debate amongst Bristol's citizens. The city council, for example, felt it important enough to give the local celebrations their own title: 'Abolition 200'. The *Bristol Evening Post* ran a whole series of articles about the bicentenary. Perhaps most significant was by Paul Stephenson, the Bristol Black activist and anti-slavery campaigner, whose article condemned Bristol's infamous past and called for the renaming of Colston Hall. The newspaper ran a follow-up feature entitled 'Soapbox' which invited readers to comment on Stephenson's views. It sparked vigorous debate, for example one respondent accused Stephenson of promoting hatred through a vitriolic attack on the memory and legacy of Edward Colston. Another called Stephenson's article a ridiculous crusade, whilst a third argued that we should accept history for what it is: dead and past. By contrast, one resident supplied information relating to the church's response to Bristol's slave trade history, in particular its campaign against recent sex-trafficking of Eastern European girls into a form of contemporary slavery. This article provoked many more local responses, showing a wide range of opinions on Bristol's slavery past.[30]

Rachel Hasted, Head of Social Inclusion at English Heritage, takes a less impassioned view when arguing: "This is the history that has often been overlooked in the past, but it is fascinating to see how many links remain in the buildings and memorials around us…this is history on our doorstep and English Heritage is committed to helping people explore their historic environment and understand that legacy."[31] For Hasted, it is not so much whether Bristolians should be ashamed of their past - after all there is no suggestion that they condone it, nor intend to repeat it - but that it remains a part of their past, and should be embraced and better understood.

In response to the call for a better understanding of the slave trade, boys at the Independent Queen Elizabeth Hospital School in Clifton built a symbolic representation of the deck of a slave ship. The idea was to encourage pupils and adults to reflect upon lost human stories behind the statistical facts of the transatlantic slave trade.[32] There were a number of events to commemorate the abolition, including a reconstruction of a riot at the New Room chapel.

Shortly after the abolition commemorations the government announced that Bristol's involvement in the slave trade would be included in the History programme for key stage 3 pupils aged 11-14 across the whole of Britain. Remarking on this inclusion, Paul Stephenson said:"It is very important that people realise that the end of slavery was not about the consent of liberal do-goodism, but was in fact about the physical rejection of the trade in enslaved Africans."[33]

The *Bristol Evening News* reported that as part of the History programme teachers will examine the question"What does it mean to be free?", as well as looking at links with emancipation and racial segregation.[34] These examples of Bristol's response to its past show that there are many contrasting views on Bristol's involvement in the slave trade and whether (or how) it should be remembered.

Conclusion

The slave trade of the seventeenth, eighteenth and nineteenth centuries had a significant financial impact throughout Britain. Bristol, thanks to its port and thriving infrastructure, benefited greatly and the legacy of this trade is everywhere, even today. No matter what the current public opinion on slavery, it remains a part of Britain's and Bristol's past. It cannot and should not be forgotten. Clearly many Bristolians today find it hard to embrace the city's infamous past, but school children are being taught to understand what happened, how it was perceived then, and how we must never let it happen again. The legacy is in the fabric of Bristol. It is also in the hearts and minds of its residents, and it is to be hoped that future generations will understand it even better.

1 J. Walvin, *A Short History of Slavery* (London: Penguin 2007), p.68.

2 Walvin, p.51.

3 M. Dresser, *Slavery Obscured. The Social History of the Slave Trade in Bristol* (Bristol: Redcliffe Press, 2001), p.28.

4 D. Richardson, *Bristol, Africa and the Eighteenth-Century Slave Trade to America* (Bristol: Bristol Record Society, 1996).

5 Dresser, p.28.

6 R. Reddie, *Abolition! The Struggle to Abolish Slavery in the British Colonies* (Oxford: Lion Hudson, 2007), p. 97-8.

7 'The Society of Merchant Venturers, History', **http://www.merchantventurers. com/about-us/history.html** (accessed 14 April 2009).

8 'The Society of Merchant Venturers, History' (accessed 14 April 2009).

9 Walvin, p. 187.

10 Dresser, p. 130.

11 'The Campaign in Bristol, Port Cities Bristol', **http://www.discoveringbristol. org.uk/showNarrative.php?sit_ id=1&narId=346&nacId=349** (accessed 14 April 2009).

12 'Thomas Clarkson', Brycchan Carey, **http://www.brycchancarey.com/abolition/** clarkson.htm (accessed 14 April 2009).

13 'In the Steps of Bristol's Abolitionists', BBC, **http://www.bbc.co.uk/bristol/ content/articles/2007/03/16/abolition_walk_ feature.shtml** (accessed 14 April 2009).

14 'Thomas Clarkson', Wikipedia **http://en.wikipedia.org/wiki/Thomas_ Clarkson** (accessed 14 April 2009).

15 Dresser.

16 'The Campaign in Bristol, Port Cities Bristol', **http://www.discoveringbristol. org.uk/showNarrative.php?sit_ id=1&narId=346&nacId=349** (accessed 14 April 2009).

17 Elizabeth Crawford, 'Women: From Abolition to the Vote, British History, Abolition of the Slave Trade 1807', **http:// www.bbc.co.uk/history/british/aboliton.** abolition_women_article_01.shtml (accessed 23 January 2009).

18 Dresser, p.142.

19 'The Society of Merchant Venturers, History', **http://www.merchantventurers. com/about-us/history.html** (accessed 14 April 2009).

20 A. Nash, 'The End of the Slave Trade, Bristol Slavery', **http://www. bristolandslavery.4t.com.the endof.html** (accessed 14 April 2009).

21 'The Slave Trade and Abolition', English Heritage, **http://www.english-heritage. org.uk/server/show/nav.17483** (accessed 14 April 2009).

22 'Bristol, the Slavery Trail', History Footsteps, Victoria County History, **http://www.victoriacountyhistory.ac.uk/ englandpast/education/legacy2.html** (accessed 27 March 2009).

23 'Exploring the Georgian House', BBC, **http://www.bbc.co.uk/Bristol/content/ articles/2007/03/27/georgianhouse_feature. shtml** (accessed 27 March 2009).

24 'Breaking the Chains', Empire and Commonwealth Museum, **http://www. empiremuseum.co.uk/exhibitions/st2007. htm** (accessed 27 March 2009).

25 'The Slave Trade and Plantation Wealth', English Heritage, **http://www.english- heritage.org.uk/server/show/nav.17487** (accessed 26 April 2009).

26 '33-35 Queen Square: Home of Captain Rogers (Trail Location 13)', Explore Bristol's Past, **http://www. englandspastforeveryone.org.uk/Counties/ Bristol/Projects/SlaveryTrail/Items/ a13QueenSquare** (accessed 27 March 2009).

27 'Parks & Green Spaces, Blaise Castle Estate', BBC, **http://www.bbc.co.uk/ bristol/content/articles/2006/03/01/blaise_ feature.shtml** (accessed 27 March 2009).

28 'The anti-slavery arch Stroud, Anti- Slavery', **http://www.anti-slaveryarch.com** (accessed 27 March 2009).

29 'Explore Bristol's Past, England's

Past for Everyone', **http://www. englandspastforeveryone.org.uk/Counties/ Bristol/Projects/SlaveryTrail/Items/ SevenStarsPub** (accessed 27 March 2009).

30 'Row over Colston Hall and Race Issue', This is Bristol, **http://www.thisisbristol. co.uk/news/Row-Colston-Hall-race-issue/article-1087632-detail/article.html** (accessed 1 July 2009).

31 'Built Legacy of Slave Trade and Abolition Revealed', English Heritage, **http://www. english-heritage.org.uk/server/show/ ConWebDoc.10711** (accessed 1 July 2009).

32 'Mission Abolition', QEH News, Issue 19 Autumn Term 2007, **http://www. qehbristol.co.uk/media/PDFs/Newsletters/ Senior/news%20issue19.pdf** (accessed 1 July 2009).

33 'Pupils to Learn about Bristol's role in Slave Trade', This is Bristol, **http://www.thisisbristol.co.uk/news/ Pupils-learn-Bristol-s-role-slave-trade/ article-292653-detail/article.html** (accessed 3 September 2009).

34 'Pupils to Learn about Bristol's role in Slave Trade', This is Bristol, **http://www.thisisbristol.co.uk/news/ Pupils-learn-Bristol-s-role-slave-trade/ article-292653-detail/article.html** (accessed 3 September 2009).

Bibliography

Dresser, *M., Slavery Obscured: The Social History of the Slave Trade in Bristol* (Bristol: Redcliffe Press, 2001)

Reddie, R., *Abolition! The struggle to abolish Slavery in the British Colonies,* (Oxford: Lion Hudson, 2007)

Richardson, D., *Bristol, Africa and the Eighteenth-century slave trade to America* (Bristol: Bristol Record Society, 1996)

Walvin, J., *A Short History of Slavery* (London: Penguin, 2007)

Websites

'The Society of Merchant Venturers, History' (accessed 14 April 2009), **http://www.merchantventurers.com/about-us/history.html**

'Abolitionism', Wikipedia (accessed 14 April 2009), **http://en.wikipedia.org/wiki/Abolitionism**

'The Campaign in Bristol, Port Cities Bristol' (accessed 14 April 2009), **http://www.discoveringbristol.org.uk/showNarrative.php?sit_ id=1&narId=346&nacId=349**

'Thomas Clarkson', Brychan Carey (accessed 14 April 2009), **http://www.brycchancarey.com/abolition/clarkson.htm**

'In the Steps of Bristol's Abolitionists', BBC (accessed 14 April 2009), **http://www.bbc.co.uk/bristol/content/articles/2007/03/16/abolition_walk_ feature.shtml**

'Thomas Clarkson', Wikipedia (accessed 14 April 2009), **http://en.wikipedia.org/wiki/Thomas_Clarkson**

E. Crawford, 'Women: From Abolition to the Vote, British History, Abolition of the slave 1807' (accessed 23 January 2009), **http://www.bbc.co.uk/history/ british/aboliton.abolition_women_article_01.shtml**

'The Society of Merchant Venturers, History' (accessed 14 April 2009), **http://www.merchantventurers.com/about-us/history.html**

A. Nash, 'The End of the Slave Trade, Bristol Slavery Date' (accessed 14 April 2009), **http://www.bristolandslavery.4t.com.the endof.htm**

'The Slave Trade and Abolition', English Heritage (accessed 14 April 2009), **http://www.english-heritage.org.uk/server/show/nav.17483**

'Bristol…the Slavery Trail', History Footsteps, Victoria County History, (accessed 27 March 2009), **http://www.victoriacountyhistory.ac.uk/englandpast/education/legacy2.html**

'Exploring the Georgian House', BBC (accessed 27 March 2009), **http://www.bbc.co.uk/Bristol/content/articles/2007/03/27/georgianhouse_feature.shtml**

'Breaking the Chains', Empire and Commonwealth Museum (accessed 27 March 2009), **http://www.empiremuseum.co.uk/exhibitions/st2007.htm**

'The Slave Trade and Plantation Wealth', English Heritage (accessed 26 April 2009), **http://www.english-heritage.org.uk/server/show/nav.17487**

'33-35 Queen Square: Home of Captain Rogers (Trail Location 13)', Explore Bristol's Past (accessed 27 March 2009), **http://www.englandspastforeveryone.org.uk/Counties/Bristol/Projects/SlaveryTrail/Items/a13QueenSquare>**

'Parks and Green Spaces, Blaise Castle Estate', BBC (accessed 27 March 2009), **http://www.bbc.co.uk/bristol/content/articles/2006/03/01/blaise_feature.shtml**

'The anti-slavery arch, Stroud, Anti-Slavery' (accessed 27 March 2009), **http://www.anti-slaveryarch.com**

'Explore Bristol's Past', England's Past for Everyone (accessed 27 March 2009), **http://www.englandspastforeveryone.org.uk/Counties/Bristol/Projects/SlaveryTrail/Items/SevenStarsPub**

'Row over Colston Hall and Race Issue', This is Bristol (accessed 1 July 2009), **http://www.thisisbristol.co.uk/news/Row-Colston-Hall-race-issue/article-1087632-detail/article.html**

'Built Legacy of Slave Trade and Abolition Revealed', English Heritage, (accessed 1 July 2009), **http://www.english-heritage.org.uk/server/show/ConWebDoc.10711**

Chapter 4

Henry Sylvester Williams:
His Achievements and Influence

by Maxim Ferreira

Who was Henry Sylvester Williams?

He was a Black man of humble origins, born in Trinidad, who was able to overcome the endemic racism of the nineteenth century in England. He qualified as a lawyer, inaugurated the Pan African Conference of 1900, and became its first General Secretary. He also wrote books and became one of the first Black local councillors in the UK.

This exemplary talent did not just drop from the sky. Rather, he was the product of a nineteenth century intellectual formation that has not been given due attention. The great Trinidadian historian C.L.R. James once observed, "The longer I live, the more I see that people are shaped to a degree that they do not yet understand by the social relations and family and other groups in which they grew up."[1] Henry Sylvester Williams' life can be divided into five sections: early years and influences in Trinidad; education of a self-made man; travels in Africa and elsewhere; the Pan African Conference in 1900; and finally, his search for a home to match his ideals and his family.

Early Years and Influences in Trinidad

Henry Williams was born in Arouca, Trinidad, in 1869, the son of a wheelwright from Barbados, and may have developed his love for Africa while growing up in Trinidad. He qualified as a primary school teacher at the age of seventeen and taught in various schools in Trinidad before immigrating to the United States in 1891.

He lived among Africans and would have known that workers were recruited from Sierra Leone after slavery to ease the labour shortage on the sugar plantations as his father worked on a sugar plantation. "Recaptives" were resettled in Trinidad from St. Helena and Rio de Janeiro.[2] Between 1841 and 1867, a total of 8385 recaptives and liberated Africans were landed in Trinidad. An exiled African prince, the son of the King of Asante, was resident with the Superintendent of the normal school where he did his teacher training.[3] He would have heard stories of Africa and been familiar with African customs as practised in Trinidad at that time. Some Africans wanted to return to their homeland. There was a movement for return to Africa by the Mandingoes but this was unsuccessful.[4] A number of European missionaries were withdrawn from Africa and from the 1870s onwards there was a move to send West Indian missionaries to Africa.

Trinidad at the time of Henry Williams' youth would have been agitating for a political franchise, as 'negroes' (Black people) and 'coloureds' (people of mixed race) were excluded from the political process even though they may have been educated and professionally trained. The island was a Crown Colony which meant the Crown controlled the executive via the Governor. All power lay in the hands of the Governor, carrying out policy laid down by the Secretary of State for the Colonies, a member of the British Parliament in London. The Legislative Council consisted of his officials and the non-officials consisted of White planters and merchants chosen by the Governor.[5] Williams would have known how Captain Baker, the Commandant of Police, tried to stop the carnival in 1881[6] and how the police shot down unarmed Indians during the Hosea festival in 1884. The subsequent investigations were damning for the government, though no charges were brought against the police. The Governor even refused to grant Emancipation Day as a holiday on 1 August 1888, but this did not stop the celebrations. In 1891 there were riots in Williams' home town of Arouca, when the police moved in to stop African drumming which was made illegal by the government.

Trinidad society at this time was extremely colour-conscious and it would have been very difficult for a Black man to succeed in that society unless he was well educated and had a 'godfather'. All the top civil servants were White, whether qualified or not. Merchants tended to be White and 'coloured'. Williams was neither, was of a humble origin, and his parents were immigrants from Barbados. He went to the local government primary school in Arouca but did not gain entrance to either Queen's Royal College or St. Mary's College in Port of Spain. This meant that his scope for progress in Trinidad was limited. In 1870 the Keenan report into the state of education in Trinidad showed that it was ineffectual and weak.[7] The teacher training was inadequate.[8] In this atmosphere, Williams was selected for a teacher training course and qualified as a third grade teacher in 1886. The newspapers of the time said that teachers were poorly paid and they found it difficult to survive.[9] The Superintendent of his school, J.J. Collens, was a member of the Temperance movement and a reformist; this greatly influenced Henry. On qualifying, he taught at various small country schools for five years and was a founder member of the Teachers' Association, of which J.J. Collens was the president.

Education of a Self-Made Man

Williams immigrated to the USA in 1891, according to C.O. Mathurin and J.R. Hooker, but there is no knowledge of his activity there except supposition. It is believed that, like many before and after, he left Trinidad to further his education and improve his circumstances. He surfaced in Canada in 1893 and again there is a lack of concrete information as to what he did there.

Williams appeared in England in1895, as a lecturer for the Church of England Temperance Society and the National Thrift Society. Williams remained a teetotaller all his life, but in the end thrift was not his strong point. During this period he met Mrs. E.V. Kinloch, a Black South African woman married to a Scottish engineer, who was a great influence on him. She knew the appalling conditions the Africans laboured under in the mines and compounds in which they were herded and kept. Williams persuaded her to speak at a large meeting he was to address. She spoke on the plight of the Blacks in Southern Africa. Williams was moved and pleased with the performance of a woman "of our race".[10] The plight of the Africans in Southern Africa and the need for a body to represent Africans provided the impetus to form the African Association on the 24 September 1897, with Williams as the honorary secretary.[11]

The stated purposes of this Association were to "encourage a feeling of unity and to facilitate friendly intercourse among Africans in general; to promote and protect the interests of all subjects claiming African descent, wholly or in part, in the British colonies and other places, especially in Africa, by circulating accurate information on all subjects affecting their rights and privileges as subjects of the British Empire, by direct appeals to the Imperial and Local Governments."[12] Some sceptics predicted that the Association would not last three months.[13] They said it was impossible for Black people to have an organisation of their own. In fact the organisation lasted about four years.

There is no information on Henry Williams continuing his education in the USA. I have found no evidence of him entering the USA in 1891 on any of the Family History websites. However both Mathurin and Hooker claim that he spent a year at Dalhousie University in Canada at the law faculty, but did not graduate. More research is needed on his movements between 1891 and 1896. In 1896 he was in London, but there is again no evidence that he attended King's College. It should be noted that he had to sit a preliminary exam to gain entrance to Gray's Inn, where he wished to train as a lawyer. This suggests that he did not have the requisite qualifications. He passed his law finals in November 1900,[14] but was not called to the bar until 1902.

All Williams' studies were financed by his own actions, unlike many others who had scholarships or wealthy parents. He was a lecturer for the Church of England Temperance Society and the National Thrift Society, but this only helped to clear his expenses. This work, however, gave him good contacts with the establishment as they saw him as respectable. He wrote a pamphlet based on two lectures, 'The Negro a Factor in the Empire' and 'The Ethiopian Eunuch',[15] and was the editor of a short-lived magazine, *The Pan-African*.[16] He was the only Black committee member of the League of Universal Brotherhood and Native Races Association, two London-based organisations involved with African issues.[17]

It is alleged that Williams was a freemason and on his death their rituals were performed.[18] I was unable to discover any concrete evidence that he was a member. The United Grand Lodge of London has not confirmed him as a member and there is no evidence in Trinidad showing him as a member, except his death notice. This is not to say he was not a member, but more research is needed. His father-in-law was a member of many masonic lodges in Hampshire. As a member of this body, many doors may have been opened to Williams. None of the historians have commented on this aspect of his life. It certainly helped him on his return to Trinidad, where he practised law until his death in 1911. But apparently it did not help his wife or children. I t seems that he was in substantial debt when he died.

Pan-African Conference 1900

Williams is given scant regard by most writers on Pan-Africanism: either a one-liner or a few lines.[19] This may be because he was the pioneer and the organisation died in 1902-3. There was no further Congress until 1919 and this was not a success. He died before his ideas could take root. Williams has nevertheless been acknowledged by C.L.R. James for his work in the 1900s.[20]

The 1900 Conference was born out of the African Association and the need for a permanent body to disseminate reliable information on Africa and Africans, and those so descended, and also to act as a political lobby. The date was chosen to coincide with the Paris Exposition which many Black people might be visiting who could also be encouraged to come to the conference. It was planned in March 1899. Booker T. Washington, the famous American writer and educator, urged as many Black Americans as possible to attend. He felt that the Conference was likely to be "one of the most effective and far reaching gatherings that had ever been held in connection with the development of the race".[21]

Williams told a gathering at the Reform Club in London on the 6 July 1900 that the Conference would be the "first occasion upon which black men would assemble in England to speak for themselves and endeavour to influence public opinion in their favour". The Conference, he added, would consider the position of Black people in South Africa and must see to it that their interests were not overlooked in any settlement of the Boer War.[22]

The Times of London reported on 24 July that a three-day Conference of "coloured" people, organised by a committee of the African Association for the discussion of the "Native Races question", had opened the previous day at Westminster Town Hall but there was no editorial comment.[23] The chairman, Bishop Alexander Walters, said that "for the first time in the history of the world black men had gathered together from all parts of the globe with the object of discussing and improving the condition of the black race."[24]

The Westminster Gazette said, "it marks the initiation of a remarkable movement in history: the Negro is at last awake to the potentialities of his future."[25] The reporter then went on to quote Williams' speech, which was a paraphrase of the objects of the new Pan-African Association.

These objects were:

1. To secure to Africans throughout the world true civil and political rights.
2. To meliorate the conditions of our brothers on the continent of Africa, America and other parts of the world.
3. To promote efforts to secure effective legislation and encourage our people in educational, industrial and commercial enterprise.
4. To foster the production of writing and statistics relating to our people everywhere.
5. To raise funds for forwarding these purposes.[26]

Positive outcomes from the Conference included the formation of a permanent body, called the Pan-African Association. A Memorial was sent to the Queen on the condition of her native subjects in South Africa who suffered "acute ill-treatment".

An Address to the Nations was also composed, which, among other things, called on the imperialist nations to respect the integrity and independence of the free 'Negro' states of Abyssinia, Liberia and Haiti. This address also produced the phrase allegedly coined by DuBois (but this is doubtful): "The problem of the Twentieth Century is the problem of the colour line."

The Queen eventually replied via her government: "Mr Chamberlain accordingly desires to assure the members of the Pan-African Conference that, in settling the lines on which the administration of the conquered territories is to be conducted, Her Majesty's Government will not overlook the interests and welfare of the native races."[27] However Joseph Chamberlain, the Colonial Secretary, regarded Blacks of the West Indies as "totally unfit for representative institutions".[28]

The Conference, although not covering its cost, was a successful event attended by over thirty delegates from Africa, the West Indies, Canada, Haiti and the USA. All historians agree that there has been no accurate report of the Conference. One significant contributor was Dadabhai Naoroji, the first Indian elected to the British Parliament. This was against a background of financial problems in his own organisation. Only Williams seemed to have been soliciting contributions both from English and Black people. Lack of financial support was soon the undoing of the Association. As C.O. Mathurin says, many of the members were students or other transient types who did not have the money or the time and were really birds of passage. One of the aims of the Association was to be financially independent, but that proved impossible.

At the turn of the century there was great social and military upheaval and people were dissatisfied with the existing structure and development of society. They were searching for new paths, yet this was the zenith of imperialism.[29] The Labour Party was formed in February 1900 and there were many other 'Pan' groups, such as Pan-Slavs and Pan-Germans. The Pan-African movement was a part of this general change in society. At the 1900 Conference the African Association's name was merged to form the Pan-African Association, but it was already being called the Pan-African Association before the meeting and it was agreed that branches should be inaugurated worldwide. Williams was appointed General Secretary at the Conference for two years, and set about inaugurating branches in Jamaica, Trinidad and the United States in 1901.[30] His trip was a success and branches were formed in Trinidad[31] and Jamaica.

Williams' visit to Trinidad coincided with an upsurge of Black consciousness. The foundations for this were laid by J.J. Thomas, the Black scholar and writer of 'Froudacity', and others including Edgar Maresse-Smith. The Black middle class responded well to this appeal to race pride. *The Mirror* (Trinidad) felt that Williams was "moving the masses and the middle class to a sense of responsibility to themselves and to the greater body of the African race".[32] But because of his other commitments and in-fighting in London, the Pan-African Association was short-lived.[33] On his return to London, Henry Williams and Bishop Walters tried to re-start the organisation but this failed.

African Travels

Henry Williams went to South Africa in 1903. He had great difficulty in being admitted to the bar, although an English barrister. In the end he was successful through strenuous efforts, but he also got involved in local politics and education and this did not endear him to the Europeans. He was boycotted by the bar in the Cape, and racial prejudice and intolerance ran so high that he thought it advisable to return to England for his own safety after a stay of fourteen months. He continued his legal practice in London. It appears his aim was to become a Member of Parliament but he failed to get a nomination as a parliamentary candidate.[34] This encouraged him for some unexplained reason to switch to local politics, and he was elected in Ward 3 of the Marylebone Borough Council on the Progressive (Liberal/ Labour) ticket.[35] He also continued to provide the liaison for various visiting African delegations.

Between 1903 and 1908 Henry Williams made many visits to Africa, the last being to Liberia and West Africa, which he visited at the invitation of President Barclay to address the bar association at a law conference. He spent a couple of weeks there and even attempted to lease land.[36] Williams was attempting to practice what he preached in returning to Africa, but this failed: maybe because of his illness, because Liberia was in turmoil, and because his wife was a white Englishwoman.[37] Illness struck him on this trip: his son later claimed that he contracted "black-water fever" and nearly died.[38] He fell foul of the British Council in Liberia through no fault of his own.[39] He then visited Sierra Leone and Guinea. It is claimed he may also have visited Nigeria, but I have found no evidence to support this.

Return to Trinidad 1908

One can only surmise that it was because of his weakened health, his failure to become a parliamentary candidate, and his young family that Henry Williams decided eventually to return to Trinidad and enter law practice in the colony. There may be another reason, that he was encouraged to leave by the British Government after the problems in Liberia and South Africa, but there is no evidence for this assumption. He was returning to a colony where he did not have the vote, either in local or national elections. Trinidad was still a Crown Colony with all power resting in London, so politically it was a huge retrograde step.

Persistence and perseverance may have been Henry Sylvester Williams' watchwords, allowing him to complete what he did in his short life, including overcoming the many difficulties of a part-time student and family man. These qualities enabled him to found the African Association and inaugurate the first Pan-African Conference. Williams regarded the Pan-African Association as the core for a world-wide concerted effort by Blacks to obtain the same political and social benefits as their white counterparts.[40]

Henry Sylvester Williams can best be summed up as an imperialist who nevertheless sought equality and justice for all people of Africa and African descent worldwide. His views were similar to Toussaint L'Overture, in that he felt it was possible to work with the imperialists. It may be said that he was a man of his time, and therefore could not foresee the break-up of empire. He was not calling for independence, but rather for equal rights within the

British Empire. He believed that English public opinion would come to the rescue and lead eventually to equal rights for Black citizens of the Empire.

Henry Williams died in Port of Spain, Trinidad, on Sunday 26 March 1911, after a serious kidney ailment brought on probably by the illness he suffered in West Africa in 1908. An obituary in the *Trinidad Mirror* said that he was greatly esteemed by all with whom he came in contact and was held in great regard by members of the profession to which he belonged, and also that his death would be felt as a distinct loss to the community. Williams was a man who had a chequered and in some respects a brilliant career, but undoubtedly his name will longest be remembered and cherished by his own people for his great interest on their behalf, which culminated in the well-known Pan-African Conference.[41]

On his death his family were left destitute, without any help from either his masonic brothers or his friends. Henry Sylvester Williams was sent into obscurity, only to be resurrected in the last forty years by the upsurge in Black History consciousness in the newly independent Third World countries. The Prime Minister of Trinidad and Tobago (The Right Honourable Patrick Manning), in a speech to the eighth annual meeting of the African Union in 2007, announced that Henry Sylvester Williams did initiate the Pan-African movement in 1900. His contribution to Pan-African Congress is now fully recognised both in Africa and the West Indies.

1 C.L.R. James, *At the Rendezvous of Victory* (London: Allison and Busby, 1984), p. 251.

2 C.O. Mathurin, *Henry Sylvester Williams and the Origins of the Pan-African Movement* (Westport: Greenwood Press, 1976), p.3.

3 Mathurin, p.7.

4 Mathurin, p. 4.

5 E. Williams, *History of the People of Trinidad and Tobago* (London: Andre Deutsch, 1962), p.13; *Public Opinion*, 26 March 1886.

6 B. Brereton, *A History of Modern Trinidad 1783-1962* (London: Heinemann ,1981).

7 *Port of Spain Gazette*, 27 October 1869.

8 D. Wood, *Trinidad in Transition. The Years After Slavery* (Oxford: Oxford University Press, 1968), p.284.

9 Newspapers – *Port of Spain Gazette* and *Trinidad Mirror*, 1870s.

10 Mathurin, p.43.

11 Mathurin, p.41.

12 Mathurin, p.40.

13 *Trinidad Mirror.*

14 Mathurin, p.79.

15 H.S. Williams, *The British Negro a Factor in the Empire.* (Brighton: W.T. Moulton, 1902).

16 *The Pan- African* is not available at the British Library, despite being catalogued. It has been lost.

17 J. Green, *Black Edwardians; Black People in Britain* 1901-1914 (London: Frank Cass, 1998), p.29; P. Fryer, *Staying Power. The History of Black People in Britain* (London: Pluto Press, 1984), p.287.

18 *Trinidad Mirror*, 29 March 1911.

19 For example, G. Fredrickson, *Black Liberation . A Comparative History of Black Ideologies in the USA and South Africa* (Oxford: Oxford University Press, 1995), p.149.

20 C.L.R. James, *At the Rendezvous of Victory* (London : Allison & Bundy, 1985), pp. 225-227, 238, 239.

21 J. Hooker, *Henry Sylvester Williams, Imperial Pan-Africanist* (London: Rex Collings,1975), p.23.

22 *The Times*, 7 July 1900.

23 *The Times*, 24 July 1900.

24 *The Times*, 24 July 1900.

25 *Westminster Gazette*, 24 July 1900.

26 Fryer, pp. 284-5.

27 Hooker, p.37.

28 Mathurin, p.71.

29 James, p.238.

30 *Trinidad Mirror*, 12 July 1901.

31 *Trinidad Mirror*, 28 June 1901.

32 *Trinidad Mirror*, 12 July 1901.

33 Hooker, p.6.

34 Hooker, p.83.

35 *Marylebone Mercury and West London Gazette*, 21 October 1906, 17 November 1906.

36 Mathurin, p.142.

37 The Liberian constitution did not allow Caucasians to become citizens and own land.

38 Hooker, p.101.

39 Mathurin, pp.143-149.

40 James, p.225.

41 *Trinidad Mirror*, 29 March 1911. Note that the paper used the term "Congress" which had not been used previously by newspapers.

Bibliography

Brereton, B., *A History of Modern Trinidad 1783-1962*
(London: Heinemann,1981)

Carmichael, G., *The History of the West Indian Islands of Trinidad and Tobago*
(London: Alvin Redman,1961)

Fryer, P., Staying Power. *The History of Black People in Britain*
(London: Pluto Press, 1984)

Gerzina, G., *Black Victorians/Black Victoriana* (New Jersey: Rutgers
University Press, 2003)

Green, J., *Black Edwardians; Black People in Britain 1901-1914*
(London: Frank Cass, 1998)

Hooker, J., *Henry Sylvester Williams, Imperial Pan Africanist*
(London: Rex Collings,1975)

James, C.L.R., *At the Rendezvous of Victory*
(London: Allison & Busby, 1984)

James, C.L.R., *Beyond a Boundary* (Kingston: Sangster Book Stores, 1963)

Mathurin, C., *Henry Sylvester Williams and the Origins of the Pan African
Movement* (Westport: Greenwood Press, 1976)

Ramdin, R., *Reimaging Britain – 500 years of Black and Asian History*
(London:Pluto Press, 1999)

Williams, E., *History of the People of Trinidad and Tobago*
(London: Andre Deutsch, 1962)

Williams, E., *British Historians and the West Indies*
(London: Andre Deutsch, 1966)

Wood, D., *Trinidad in Transition: The Years After Slavery*
(Oxford: Oxford University Press,1968)

Newspapers

The Times	London
Marylebone Mercury and West London Gazette	London
Westminster Gazette	London
Rochester, Chatham and Gillingham Journal	Kent
POS Gazette	Trinidad
The Mirror	Trinidad
Public Opinion	Trinidad
San Fernando Gazette	Trinidad

Chapter 5

Claudia Jones

by Elnora Latchman

Claudia Jones was a major activist in the struggle for equality and justice for the world's poor and exploited people, although many people have not heard about her. Claudia's life was one of personal battle with illness brought about by poverty and persecution, but despite these adversities, Claudia persevered as a devoted freedom fighter until her death in December 1964.

Despite racism and persecution in the United States, Claudia became a prominent leader in the struggle against racism and chauvinism in the USA which eventually led to her imprisonment and deportation to the United Kingdom. On arrival in Britain she continued to devote her remarkable abilities to fighting for equality for immigrants to Britain and actively supported the struggle of anti-colonialists and Pan-Africanists in this country. In Britain Claudia is best remembered for starting the *West Indian Gazette* newspaper, the rallying point for many freedom fighters and the voice of protest against racial discrimination in everyday life and in Government legislation; and also as the founder of the Notting Hill Carnival.

Early years

Claudia's parents Mr and Mrs Cumberbatch emigrated from Barbados to Trinidad, where she and her three sisters were born during the time of British colonial rule. Following World War 1 and the collapse of the Trinidad economy, the family immigrated to the Harlem area of New York, USA, in search of a better life. Claudia and her sisters attended school in Harlem and before leaving school, Claudia had earned President Roosevelt's Good Citizenship Award.

The Cumberbatch family entered the USA at a time of global economic struggle leading up to the period that is generally known as the Great Depression (1930s). Following the abolition of slavery, white businessmen and industrialists, with the support of Government legislation, kept African Americans and poor Whites in a near-slavery situation by paying the lowest possible wages. Consequently, Mrs Cumberbatch died from overwork five years after arrival in New York. Mr Cumberbatch was forced to take the only job available to him - caretaker of a run-down block of apartments where the family had to live in the damp, unsanitary basement apartment deprived of proper ventilation. As a result of these conditions, Claudia contracted tuberculosis and spent a year of her school life in hospital, leaving her with a weak heart and lungs and lifelong health problems.

When Claudia left school, she was offered only the most menial and low-paid jobs, despite her intelligence and ambitious character. Her experiences of racism and chauvinism motivated her to join the struggle for racial, economic and gender equality.

Decision to Join the Communist Party

At the age of eighteen years Claudia read reports of the active support given by the Communist Party to the defence of nine young Black men who had been charged, without evidence, with the rape of two white girls. Claudia learnt of the Communist Party's campaign against the Italian occupation of Ethiopia and its active participation in the fight for social, economic and political rights for Black people in America. She learned that racial discrimination was a criminal offence in the Soviet Union since 1922.

In Claudia's own words: "It was out of my Jim Crow experiences as a young negro woman, experiences likewise born of working class poverty that led me to join the young Communist League and to choose the philosophy of my life, the science of Marxism-Leninism – that philosophy that not only rejects racist ideas, but is the anti-thesis of them" (Buzz Johnson, p.7).

Claudia the Activist

After joining the Communist Party of the USA, Claudia Cumberbatch became Claudia Jones. While working as a technician with a black newspaper Claudia attended courses and wrote articles for the Young Communist League's Weekly Review. Within a few years her talents led to appointment as Chair of the National Council of the Young Communist League and in 1941 she was appointed as National Director and Education Officer for New York. Claudia wrote articles for the 'Negro Affairs' section of the *Daily Worker* (the Communist Party's publication) and became a prominent speaker and campaigner for equal rights for Black Americans, women and oppressed people throughout the world. Subsequently Claudia became Associate Editor of the *Daily Worker* and then Editor.

Claudia's outstanding abilities were demonstrated by her campaign speeches in various parts of the United States against oppression. She supported and participated in the work of trade unionists, the women's movement founded by Elizabeth Gurley Flynn, movements for freedom from colonial rule, anti-apartheid in South Africa, as well as working with the National Negro Congress and Southern Youth Congress. Claudia also joined in the campaign for peace and unity, and against the manufacture and stockpiling of war weapons of mass destruction, especially after America had dropped atomic bombs in Japan.

Claudia was appointed to the National Committee of the Communist Party in America, where she worked alongside other well-known political activists such as Paul and Esslander Robeson, George Padmore, Ben Davis, C.L.R. James, W.E.B. DuBois and Elizabeth Gurley Flynn. Many of these friends and colleagues maintained a relationship with her after deportation to Britain. Despite continued illness, Claudia's activities included helping to organise and lead protests against the killing of black youths in the South and across America, and campaigning for an end to the oppression of women and for the release of arrested colleagues, including her close friend Ben Davis.

Many Black Americans left the Communist Party during and after the Second World War because of the Party's withdrawal of support for anti-colonialists. This was a direct consequence of the different relationship between Russia and its new war-time allies. However Claudia remained loyal and tried to attract new membership due to her strong beliefs in the Marxist-Leninist way of life. Her open criticisms of prejudices and chauvinisms within the Party demonstrated her strong views that the party should lead by example.

Persecution, Arrest and Deportation

Many people will be know of the history period of 'McCarthy witch-hunts', which took place in America in the 1940s and 1950s. As a leading member of the Communist Party, Claudia was one of many people who were persecuted by the Federal Bureau of Investigation. Along with many other foreign-born people and Communist Party members, Claudia was arrested on 19 January 1948 and taken to Ellis Island, despite being ill at the time. Following her release on bail, Claudia went on a speaking tour of twelve American cities.

Claudia was re-arrested in early 1950 and again taken to Ellis Island. Found Guilty of "plotting to overthrow the government by Force" in December 1950, Claudia was released on bail while an appeal was submitted. On the night of 20 June 1951, seventeen Party members including Claudia were again arrested. The charge against Claudia was that she had broken her bail conditions by publishing an article for International Women's Day. The trials of Claudia and many of her colleagues took place in 1953, after which another appeal was made to the Supreme Court. Claudia's final sentence was prison for one year and a day, plus a fine of two thousand dollars.

Unfortunately the Supreme Court refused to hear the appeal and Claudia was confined to a segregated prison, without access to proper medical care or dietary needs. Many individuals and organisations in America and abroad including the Caribbean Labour Congress and school children campaigned for Claudia's release, but to no avail. Only when a judge threatened to release Claudia did the prison authorities comply with her dietary requirements and moved her to a non-segregated section of the prison near to her comrade Elizabeth Gurley Flynn. Meanwhile, the American government implemented a deportation order, on release, despite Claudia's worsening health. On release from prison Claudia was reluctantly allowed a stay of one month to obtain medical treatment before her forced departure to Britain. A farewell party was attended by many of her colleagues (those who were not imprisoned), including Paul Robeson.

Life in Britain

Claudia Jones arrived in Britain in December 1955. After staying with exiled colleagues Mae and John Williamson, then Charlie and Mikki Doyle, she finally found a flat in South London owned by Reverend Hewlett Johnson, the Communist Dean of Canterbury. She only knew a few people who, like herself, had been deported from America. In addition to her financial difficulties, the Communist Party allocated Claudia a job as a typist at the China News Agency, completely disregarding her proven oratory and writing talents. Recognising the underlying racism within the party and outside, Claudia wrote urging the party to take the lead in fighting racism, for economic and social equality for immigrants in Britain and for independence of colonial countries.

True to her indomitable spirit, Claudia refused to be daunted by the cold attitude of the British Communist Party. Claudia established links with organisations outside the Communist Party where she could contribute to the on-going struggles for racial equality in Britain and abroad, and independence of Caribbean, African and Asian countries.

The Party appointed her to the West Indies Committee where she worked alongside Amy Ashwood Garvey, Pearl Prescod, Frances Ezzrecco and many outstanding West Indians, Africans and Asians. Claudia also joined the London Branch of the Caribbean Labour Congress (which had campaigned for her release from prison) and assisted with publishing its newspaper, *Caribbean News*, until it ceased in 1956. The paper campaigned for an independent West Indian Federation to govern the West Indies from a Trinidad base. She was one of the founder members of the West Indian Students and Workers Association, which joined the campaign against apartheid in South Africa and against colonial rule. Claudia also formed strong links with Asian members of the Communist Party, particularly with A. Manchanda (Manu) with whom she founded the Indian Workers Association.

Throughout all her various activities, Claudia continued to have bouts of illness and hospitalisation, no doubt aggravated by her poverty. Old friends and colleagues in America sent her small amounts of money to assist whenever they could. It must have been a welcome relief to be invited to the South of France in late 1957 for a short holiday, where she apparently met Pablo Picasso.

The West Indian Gazette

The *West Indian Gazette* was first published under the auspices of the West Indian Workers and Students Association, with Claudia as the editor. The first publication in March 1958 from premises at 250 Brixton Road was a one-page flyer which proved to be popular, although mostly delivered by hand. Within a few months, Fascists broke in and trashed the Gazette's office. This, along with the race riots in Notting Hill and Coventry in the summer of 1958, reminded Claudia of her experiences in America and prompted her to action.

Undaunted by violence and under extreme financial constraints, Claudia made the *Gazette* into a rallying point for many political and human rights activists and used it to publicise campaigns and protest activities. Claudia was one of the founding members of the Inter-Racial Friendship Co-ordinating

1 N. Longmate, *The Home Front. An Anthology 1938-1945* (London: Chatto and Windus,1981), p. xi.

2 D. Dabydeen, J Gilmore and C Jones, (Oxford: Oxford University Press (2007), p.xxvii.

3 R. Mackay, *The Test of War* (London: UCL Press, 1999), p.15.

4 Wikipedia. **www.en.wikipedia.org/wiki/ British_Empire** (accessed 20 April 2009).

5 H. Smith, 'Black History and Two World Wars'. Guest Lecture at University of Northampton, 4 November 2008.

6 B. Bousquet and C. Douglas, *West Indian Women at War. British Racism in World War II* (London: Lawrence and Wishart, 1991), p. 98.

7 P. Fryer, *The History of Black People in Britain* (London: Pluto Press, 1985), p.356.

8 Bousquet, p.27.

9 Bousquet, p.3.

10 Bousquet, p.127.

11 Bousquet, p.133.

12 Bousquet, p.134.

13 Bousquet, p.25.

14 D. Jarrett-Macauley, *The Life of Una Marson, 1905-1965* (Manchester: Manchester University Press,1998), p.144.

15 Dabydeen, p.288.

16 Dabydeen, p.436.

17 D. Jarrett-Macauley, Interview on Women's Hour, BBC Radio 4, 3 March 2009.

18 Southwark Council Site, **www.southwark. gov.uk/Uploads/FILE_41346.pdf** (accessed 20 April 2009).

19 Jarrett-Macauley, p.145.

20 Bousquet, p.4.

21 Bousquet, p.147.

22 Dabydeen, p.288.

23 Jarrett-Macauley, p.154.

24 BBC News Website, **www.news.bbc. co.uk/1/hi/england/london/7931056.stm** (accessed 20 April 2009).

25 Tales Website, www.tales.co.uk/HUTCH2. HTML (accessed 20 April 2009).

26 The Stage News Website, **www.thestage. co.uk/news/newsstory.php/21357/wartime- entertainer-hutch-remembered-in-c4** (accessed 20 April 2009).

27 'High Society's Favourite Gigolo', Channel 4, Maroon Productions, shown on 25 November 2008.

28 Bousquet, p.27.

29 Dabydeen, p.437.

30 A. Marwick, *The Home Front. The British and the Second World War* (London: Thames and Hudson,1976), p.99.

31 Fryer, p.359.

32 Mass Observation Records. Archived on microfiche at the University of Northampton.

33 E. Hopkins, *A Social History of the English Working Classes, 1815-1914* (London: Edward Arnold, 1979), p.267.

34 Bousquet, p.141.

35 Dabydeen, p. vii.

36 Dabydeen, p. vii.

37 Northampton Black History Project, **http://www.northants-black-history.org.uk/ documents/june2005.pdf** (accessed 20 April 2009).

38 Dabydeen, p.vii.

39 BBC News Website, **www.news.bbc. co.uk/1/hi/england/london/7931056.stm** (accessed 20 April 2009).

39 'High Society's Favourite Gigolo', Channel 4 TV.

Bibliography

Adi, H., *West Africans in Britain 1900-1960. Nationalism, Pan-Africanism and Communism* (London: Lawrence and Wishart, 1998)

Bousquet, B. and Douglas, C., *West Indian Women at War. British Racism in World War II* (London: Lawrence and Wishart, 1991)

Dabydeen, D., Gilmore, J., and Jones, C., eds., *The Oxford Companion to Black British History* (Oxford: Oxford University Press, Oxford, 2007)

Fryer, P., *The History of Black People in Britain* (London: Pluto Press, 1985)

Hopkins, E., *A Social History of the English Working Classes, 1815-1945* (London: Edward Arnold, 1979)

Jarrett-Macauley, D., *The Life of Una Marson, 1905-1965* (Manchester: Manchester University Press, 1998)

Longmate, N., Ed., *The Home Front. An Anthology 1938 1945* (London: Chatto and Windus, 1981)

Mackay, R., *The Test of War* (London: UCL Press, 1999)

Marwick, A., *The Home Front. The British and the Second World War* (London: Thames and Hudson, 1976)

Smith, H., ed., *Britain in the Second World War. A Social History* (Manchester: Manchester University Press, 1996)

Mass Observation Records. Archived on microfiche at the University of Northampton

Hugh Smith, Guest Lecturer, University of Northampton, 4 November 2008

'High Society's Favourite Gigolo', Channel 4, Maroon Productions, shown on 25 November 2008

BBC News Website (accessed 20 April 2009), **http://news.bbc.co.uk/1/hi/uk/3705139.stm**

BBC Radio 4 Website (accessed 8 March 2009), **http://www.bbc.co.uk/radio4/womanshour/2003_02_wed_03.shtml"http://www.bbc.co.uk/radio4/womanshour/2003_02_wed_03.shtml.**

Imperial War Museum Website (accessed 20 April 2009), **http://www.iwm.org.uk/upload/package/11/together/women/Lilian_Bader.pdf**

Ministry of Defence Website (accessed 20 April 2009), **http://www.wewerethere.defencedynamics.mod.uk/ww2/l_bader.html**

Northampton Black History Project Website (accessed 20 April 2009), **http://www.northants-black-history.org.uk/documents/winter2005.pdf"http://www.northants-black-history.org.uk/documents/winter2005.pdf** and http://www.

northants-black-history.org.uk/documents/june2005.pdf

Oxford Dictionary of National Biography (accessed 20 April 2009), **www.oxforddnb.com/articles** on Leslie Hutchinson and Una Marson

TALES website (accessed 20 April 2009), **http://tales.co.uk/HUTCH2.HTML**

The Stage News Website (accessed 20 April 2009), **http://www.thestage.co.uk/news/newsstory.php/21357/wartime-entertainer-hutch-remembered-in-c4**

Chapter 7

West Indian Soldiers in World War II

by Hugh Smith

Introduction

It is a little known fact that people of the West Indies took part in World War II (1939-1945), both in terms of actual fighting and providing material support. Cotton, sugar, tobacco, minerals and precious metals were exported to help the Allied war effort. During World War II the United Kingdom also received financial support from all the islands in the Caribbean. It is my belief that if these facts were taught to all students, regardless of race or colour, in Britain it would help to promote a positive image of Black people in this country. This chapter will also highlight the contributions made by British-born Black people of Afro-Caribbean heritage; however it will not include the enormous contributions made to the war effort by Africans, Afro-Americans and the other colonies of the British Empire.

There are a number of examples of wartime propaganda posters emphasizing the role played by the British Empire in World War II. One poster shows Asian and Black men carrying weapons in support of the UK and the slogan reads *"TOGETHER"*. Another poster shows Black men working in a quarry, and reads *"Help the West Indies to work for VICTORY"*. It is likely that these posters were displayed in the Caribbean to enlist the help of its peoples.[1]

Over 10,000 West Indians took part in WWII. They fought in campaigns in Burma, Malaya and North Africa. The actual numbers that took part in Europe is unknown as records may have been destroyed or other factors like racism may have played a part in keeping this fact out of sight. Many Afro-Caribbeans growing up in Britain have never heard of Black people playing a role in the victory over Germany. In today's Britain, the action of not including people of colour in the story of protecting Britain in a time of need would be deemed as institutionalised racism.

Dr Moody had six children. One of his sons, Charles, became the first Black commissioned officer in the British Army during the war period. He served in the Queen's Own Royal West Kent Regiment. At the end of the war, Charles became a major having fought in several campaigns in Africa, Italy and Egypt. He left Britain for Jamaica and served in the Jamaican Territorial Army, where he attained the rank of Colonel in 1961.

In one of the displays highlighted in the 'Keep Smiling Through: Black Londoners on the Home Front 1939 to 1945' exhibition at the Cuming Museum in Southwark, Dr Moody mentions that nine and a quarter million pounds sterling was given to Britain by the islands of the West Indies. Between the years 1939 and 1945 Trinidad exported over 400 million gallons of oil, and during the same period, Guyana exported nearly 2 million tons of bauxite for the war effort.[16] *Whose Freedom?* lists the number of Caribbeans killed at 236, 17 missing, 265 wounded and 96 taken as prisoners of war. It is very likely that the figure of people who perished is much higher, as it does not include the Caribbean men and women who died in merchant shipping attacks by German U-Boats.

Connie Mark joined the Auxiliary Territorial Service in 1943 in Jamaica. In the following quote she mentions how the war affected people in the Caribbean: "Of course we had hundreds of thousands of West Indians fighting the war. I went to a mixed school to do my commercial course and sat next to a young man who later joined the RAF. I saw his name on the list of war dead".[17]

Paratrooper Ronald Henrigues from Jamaica served with the 1st British Airborne Division, and was involved in the assault on Arnhem. He was wounded by machine gun fire and captured and taken prisoner by the Germans.[18] The film *The Longest Day* (1962) highlights this attack by Allied Forces.

Even in the field of entertainment in London, Ken 'Snakehips' Johnson from Guyana was well sought after and played on BBC Radio broadcasts in 1940. Unfortunately, he and members of his band were killed in a bomb blast during a performance at the Café de Paris in 1941.[19]

The first Black female programme maker for the BBC during the war period was Una Marson, who arrived in Britain in 1932 from Jamaica. She was secretary of the League of Coloured People and focused on Black women's rights. She also hosted the BBC Radio program 'West Indies Calling'. A video of the programme can be seen at the exhibition 'Keep Smiling Through: Black Londoners on the Home Front 1939 to 1945' (Cuming Museum, Southwark London). It is said that Una Marson was "widely respected, she counted such literary figures as George Orwell and T.S. Eliot among her BBC colleagues."[20]

Racism

Marika Sherwood's book *Many Struggles* documents many examples of what West Indians of Afro-Caribbean heritage had to face, not only in their home countries, but also in their willingness to help the 'Mother Country'. It appears that the 'Mother Country' was not always very grateful. The following was being said as late as 1944 by the Foreign and Colonial Office in Britain: "We must keep up the fiction of there being no colour bar while actually only those blacks with special qualifications are likely to be accepted for enlistment."[21]

In November 1939 the Foreign and Colonial Office informed its consular offices that "only offers of service from white British subjects should be considered".[22] It does seem that the UK government at the time still held the view that after the war all would go back to the way it was, and that Britain would once again rule the colonies.

The colour bar was widely practiced by the Royal Navy and the Royal Air Force. In the Air Force Act, Section 95, it is stated that "enlistment was only open to men of pure European descent".[23] The colour of one's skin also played a role. For example two hundred West Indian women sent to serve in the Auxiliary Territorial Service in Washington, USA were White. Why this happened is unclear, it could be related to the colour bar or to ensure the USA did not have a reason to reject the recruits in question. In 1943, Learie Constantine, the world famous West Indies cricketer, booked a room for himself and his family at the Imperial Hotel in London, while on official duty for the Ministry of Labour. However, they were refused a room. He later sued the hotel for damages and won his case. Even some members of the clergy had a say on race relations during the war. The Bishop of Salisbury advised that "On no account should young women make acquaintance and take walks with soldiers of African blood."[24]

In the booklet titled *Why Have We Been Forgotten?* A.K. Titus-Glover states that "Among a group of evacuees being sent to Blackpool, were two little coloured boys. Nobody wanted them, house after house refused to have them. Finally a very poor old lady of 70 years volunteered to care for them. She gave them a good supper, bathed them and put them to bed. As she folded their clothes she discovered two letters addressed to the person who adopted them, each letter contained a five pound note."[25] The sentiments felt by British born Black people can be found at the 'Keep Smiling Through: Black Londoners on the Home Front 1939 to 1945' exhibition. Some captions highlight the feelings, experiences and treatment of young Black children during their evacuation from London. One photograph shows a solitary small boy struggling to carry his own suitcase, while another shows a well-dressed Black mother and daughter joining the crowds of evacuees.

In *Our War*, Dudley Thompson from Jamaica mentions that he had to prove Hitler wrong when Hitler described Jews and negroes as "Semi anthropoid and undeveloped human beings".[26] This shows that race was a factor in the war and a reason why some wanted to fight. *Whose Freedom?* confirms the same point.

According to Stephen Bourne in his book *Speak Of Me As I Am*, a Charter for Coloured Peoples was drawn up. It called for "full self government for the colonies and insisted that racial discrimination in Britain be made illegal: the same economic, educational, legal and political rights shall be enjoyed by all persons, male and female, whatever their colour." [27] The words used sound like they belong in a charter for the United Nations on human rights, and they are clearly a direct response to the colour bar.

Cy Grant mentions the picture taken of him by the Germans after he was shot down and captured over Holland. The picture has a caption which states "RAF had to resort to the recruitment of people of unknown or indeterminate race to fight their wars for them."[28] This illustrates how the Nazis viewed peoples of colour and is an indication of their ideas on race.

In *Stolen Legacy*, George James explains the origin of prejudices that may have influenced the treatment meted out to people of colour in wartime Britain. James attribute this to the "theft of the African legacy by the Greeks [which] led to the erroneous world opinion that the African people are naturally backward. This is the misrepresentation that has become the basis of race prejudice, which has affected all the people of colour."[29] This sums up the basis for the colour bar and the restrictions placed on West Indians joining the Armed Forces of the UK. It also highlights the attitudes and views held by the British establishment at the time, and even to some extent today.

Achievements and Honours

It is not widely known that West Indians achieved honours during, and long after the end of, World War II. For example Cy Grant mentions that 103 West Indian aircrew received decorations.[30] Squadron Leader Ulric Cross, received the DSO and DFM. Flying Officer Errol Walton Barrow, ex-Prime Minister of Barbados, has his birthday celebrated as a public holiday on 21 January every year in Barbados. Flight Sergeant Lincoln Orville Lynch of 102 Squadron, RAF, was awarded the DFM for his skill as an air gunner in bombing missions. Ulric Cross and Learie Constantine can be seen making a radio broadcast in the BBC propaganda film 'West Indies Calling'. Both men are very impressive in what they have to say about their experiences in the war effort.[31] Sam King, mentioned earlier, later went on to become the first Black Mayor of Southwark in London. Dr Harold Moody was honoured with an English Heritage Blue Plaque at his former home, 164 Queen's Road, Peckham, London.

Connie Mark mentions that war memorials can be found in towns and villages throughout the West Indies. She goes on to explain how a friend returning to the Caribbean from England lost her life during a torpedo attack on her ship. Connie Mark was awarded the BEM and she also received an MBE for her work in the community in London; she passed away in June 2007. In a comment made on her passing Clive Soley, Lord Soley of Hammersmith, stated that "Connie was a remarkable woman of generosity, warmth and commitment, her photographic record of the contribution to the war effort by so many is a testimony to her love of Britain and the Caribbean."[32]

Before leaving the RAF, Lilian Bader gained the rank of Leading Aircraft Woman. Lilian had two sons, one of whom went on to join the RAF and served as a helicopter pilot during the troubles in Northern Ireland. She states "All in all I think we've given back more to this country than we've received."[33]

In November 2002 the Queen belatedly opened the Memorial Gates at Constitution Hill in London, to honour those from Africa, Asia and the West Indies who died in the World Wars. Four massive white pillars list the names of former British colonies which contributed to the war effort. Meanwhile, in James Park, Scarborough, Tobago one can also see a memorial to the soldiers that took part in World War 1 and World War II. A sculptured head surmounts a black stone tablet listing the names of servicemen and women, while a

I was amazed at how Bob was playing with a football at the bottom of the spiral stairs in the house. Later on I found out he had a passion for football. It was a day to remember, to meet two world stars at once from Jamaica.

During this period, I was honoured to be in a party of guests and reggae artists accompanying Bob Marley to visit Haile Selassie's son and grandchildren at a function in Swiss Cottage, London. My friend Jackie and I often reminisce and have laughter about that evening. This memory in particular always brings back the laughter. Because we wanted to look the part for this 'cultural event', we asked Jackie's African neighbour to help us to dress in 'African style' with the head wrap to match the dress. But on reaching Swiss Cottage, we observed that Haile Selassie's grandchildren were dressed in the modern English style of straight cord trousers! I can remember saying to Jackie, "I hope they do not come and start talking in an African language, thinking we are from Africa direct."

I also saw Bob Marley four times in concert, the first three times as a teenager in the mid 1970s: at the Fantasia, Kings Heath, Northampton; at the Bamboo Club, St Paul's, Bristol; then at the National Stadium, Kingston, Jamaica. The final time I saw him was at the Rainbow Theatre, Finsbury Park, London. Here again I was honoured, with others, to be a guest of Bob Marley's. A group of us left from his Kings Road residence to the Rainbow Theatre. It was the second time I had seen the 'I Threes', a female group with Judy Mowatt, Rita Marley and Marcia Griffith, perform: they were Bob Marley and the Wailers' backing vocal group.

It was a magical night. The atmosphere was electric and there were crowds outside with no tickets to enter. It was a sit-down affair where I felt restricted, as it was the first time I had been to hear reggae music and been seated. Halfway through the performance people stood up and began dancing, which was great! It was a revelation to me to see 75 per cent of the audience were White people. I learnt from then onwards to always buy one's ticket in advance. Bob's concert taught me never to be caught out in the cold. That was the last time I saw Bob Marley, and today I can relive it memorably and savour that night over thirty years ago like it was yesterday.

His music united me with others who enjoyed his musical lyrics, as I travelled extensively all over the UK to hear reggae music with my late brother Eddie White and his sound system, known nationally as 'Count Shelley Sound' from Northampton, which he owned in partnership with three other friends.

I did not realise that Bob had made an impression on my life until I reflected, but as I am writing I can see his time on earth helped me to journey through my life. Bob's music gave me confidence. I played his music a lot, which I varied to suit my moods. His music gave me hope and encouragement, and it still does. It was shortly after qualifying as a nurse that I had the courage to join the Northamptonshire Police Constabulary as the first African Caribbean Police Officer. Bob Marley made me feel prouder to be Black. I felt free to express my opinions, and his music helped me to meditate. It also opened my mind, allowing me to look introspectively.

After Bob died I went on a pilgrimage to Nine Miles, Saint Ann, Jamaica - his birth and resting place - to pay homage. Bob Marley made things happen for the better, both in the music business and as a philanthropist. He supported hundreds of people financially as well as his own family. He gave the credits of his music 'No Woman No Cry' to a disabled friend. He was a man of the people who dealt in 'one love'. Bob left a very special message of love in my heart, and he is one of my Legends.

Bob's Roots and the Development of Reggae

Robert Nesta Marley was born on 6 February 1945 in the village of Nine Miles in St Ann Parish, Jamaica. His mother, the late Cedella Booker, was a Black Jamaican from Saint Ann, and his father, Norval Marley, was a White Jamaican from the parish of Clarendon, Jamaica, with English roots in Liverpool. They were married, but Norval's mother did not approve of the marriage, resulting in them living apart. Bob was very close to his maternal grandfather Omeriah Malcolm, who farmed in the local area of Nine Miles and was well respected by all who knew him.

When Bob was ten years old, his father died; shortly after, he joined his mother who had moved to Trench Town, Kingston, Jamaica. In 1955 Trench Town was very rough. The dirt roads, shanty houses and crime made it a ghetto. It was here that Bob earned the name 'Tuff Gong' (this means having physical strength). He learnt to defend himself and overcame the racial abuse due to his parentage. This nickname later became the name of his Recording Studio, Tuff Gong Music, in Kingston, Jamaica.

Trench Town was Bob's foundation for his music. This is where it began: a place where some of his lyrics were composed and also a place he sang about. One of the songs which became greatly known was 'No Woman No Cry'. A chorus of the song went like this: "I remember when we used to sit in a government yard in Trench Town… In this bright future, you can't forget your past… Oh, little darling…oh my little sister… don't shed no tears… No Woman, No Cry'.[1]

Bob's musical journey was not an easy ride. He endured the hardship of poverty as a youth. He tried welding as a trade, but returned to music following an eye injury. He courted and married Alfarita Constania Anderson, known as Rita Marley, in 1966 - just before flying off to the USA to live with his Mum in Delaware, so as to make some money. On two occasions Bob went and worked in Delaware, but the weather did not agree with him. It was too cold, and also he did not wish to be drafted into the Vietnam War.

Back in Kingston, Jamaica, to get a start in the studio and to make a tune in those days, you had to eat humble pie and be willing to work hard. Bob grew up with Bunny Wailer. Their parents had a relationship and they shared a sister. Bob and Bunny also shared the love of music, and with the addition of Peter MacIntosh, Beverley Kelso, Cherry Smith and Junior Braithwaite the backbone of the famous original Wailers was formed. In 1966, the ladies and Junior left the Wailers. Bob had Joe Higgs, a Rasta Elder, as a mentor and there were many others who joined the band throughout, Joe Higgs being one of these musicians.

Before Bob became 'Bob and The Wailers', his group was first called 'The Teenagers'. They sang 'Ska' and 'Rock Steady'. They changed names twice before becoming known as 'The Wailers' – having been known previously as 'The Wailing Rudeboys' and 'The Wailing Wailers'. The first song Bob wrote and sang was 'Judge Not'(Island Label, 1961). This opportunity came about by Bob meeting the reggae singer Desmond Dekker, when they both worked as welders. Desmond introduced him to Jimmy Cliff (a reggae artist). This led to a meeting with music producer Leslie Kong, whose main business was in making and selling ice cream. He recognised Bob's musical talent and gave him his first step into his music career.

In 1975 Bob saw his music make a "mark on the US and UK charts… saw the fulfilment of his promise as an artist …and the promise of reggae music…a music he felt could have an international appeal". [2] Also on their European tours "they filled stadiums with over 100,000 people".[3] Bob's life with his music had put Jamaica and reggae music internationally on the map.

Bob Marley became known as the 'King of Reggae Music'. Reggae music evolved out of a combination of different Jamaican folk music including

'Ska'; 'Rock Steady' and 'Blue Beat' during the1960s. Lee Scratch Perry was instrumental at the start of reggae music, and also as a producer who helped Bob and the Wailers fine-tune their original musical style. Reggae is a music that has a drum bass and an array of other instruments, such as a guitar and organ. There are words to accompany the harmony, usually depicting the local news of the time. For example, 'Zimbabwe' was written and sung by Bob whilst in Ethiopia on an extended holiday. You can also have instrumental reggae where there are no words, just music. Another form of instrumental reggae is dub, which has a very heavy bass line.

Chris Blackwell, a wealthy White Jamaican living in London in the 1970s, was a music producer and owner of the Islands Record Company. He became famous in the 1960s when he produced Millie Small, a young Black Jamaican girl, who sang 'My Boy Lollipop' that went to number two in the British Musical Pop Charts (Top of the Pops). Bob and the Wailers visited Chris to get some money in advance to produce a record. Chris trusted Bob and gave him four thousand pounds, and as a result Bob Marley and the Wailers produced their first best-selling album, 'Catch a Fire'. This was followed by the album 'Burning', which featured a track called 'I Shot the Sheriff'. A cover version recorded by Eric Clapton became number one in the American music chart.

Chris bought the rights to release Bob and the Wailers from a contract with Simms, another record producer, to enable them to further their musical development. He also aided them with premises in Jamaica, on Hope Road, Kingston, where they lived and had a recording studio. This is where Bob Marley's Museum is situated today. Initially when they met, Chris enquired why they chose the name 'The Wailers'. Bob replied, "We call ourselves de Wailers because we started out crying."[4]

Bob Marley was a member of the Rastafarian faith. He was well known as a believer in Jah and in the use of cannabis, which was an integral part of his life. In 1980 Bob was baptised in the Christian Ethiopian Orthodox faith.

The Support of His Wife

They say "behind every successful man is a great woman", which is definitely the case with Bob and Rita Marley. Many would argue that Bob had many other women in his life. This, to me, makes Rita even greater. She stuck to her wedding vows through sickness and health, till death do us part. Not many women would have been able to stand a quarter of the tribulations that Rita endured through having Bob as her husband. They spent time apart on

1   Rita Marley, with Hettie Jones, *No Woman, No Cry. My Life With Bob Marley* (New York: Hyperion, 2004), front cover.

2   Kwame Dawes, *Bob Marley, Lyrical Genius* London, (London: Sanctuary Publishers, 2002), p.160.

3   K. Dawes, 161.

4   Timothy White, *Catch a Fire. The Life of Bob Marley* (London: Elm Tree Books/ Hamiliton Ltd Publisher, 2006), p.250.

5   Rita Marley on 'Special Saturday Night Sequence', BBC Radio One, May 1984.

6   Don Taylor on 'Special Saturday Night Sequence', BBC Radio One, May 1984.

7   Interview with Clifford Gulley, Northampton, January 2008.

8   Interview with Andrew Bryan, Northampton, March 2008.

9   Interview with Stewart Gordon, Northampton, January 2008.

10 Maxi Priest on 'Special Saturday Night Sequence', May 1984.

11 Bob Marley and The Wailers, 'War', 1975.

12 Neville Garrick on 'Special Saturday Night Sequence', May 1984.

13 Interview with Robin Small, Kingston, Jamaica, January 2008.

14 Interview with Jackie Edwards, London, April 2008.

Bibliography

Books

Davies, S., *Bob Marley, Conquering Lion of Reggae*
(New Jersey: Plexus Publishing,1994)

Dawes, K., *Bob Marley, Lyrical Genius* (London: Sanctuary, 2002)

Johnson, H. and J. Pines, *Reggae Deep Roots Music*
(Saline: Proteus Publishing, 1982)

Marley, R. and H. Jones, *No Woman, No Cry. My Life with Bob Marley*
(New York: Hyperion, 2004)

McCann, I., *The Complete Guide to the Music of Bob Marley*
(London: Omnibus Press, 1994)

White, T., *Catch a Fire. The Life of Bob Marley*
(New York: Holt Paperbacks, 2006)

Newspaper articles

'Wailer Refuses to Wait in Vain for £60m, of Marley's Royalties',
The Times, 17 March 2006

'The Legend', Flyer Newspaper, **www.flyernewspaper.com**

'Stephen Marley Takes 2008 Grammy with Mind Control',
The Weekly Gleaner, 18-24 February 2008

'Trench Town Culture Yard Fights for Survival', *The Weekly Gleaner*,
18-24 February 2008

'A Chat with Mama Marley', *The Weekly Gleaner*, 18-24 February 2008

'Balling Down Babylon', *The Weekly Gleaner*, 18-24 February 2008

Radio broadcast

BBC Radio One, 'Special Saturday Night Sequence', May 1984

Interviews

Mr Clifford Gulley – Northampton, January 2008

Mr Stewart Gordon 'Topper' – Northampton, January 2008

Mr Robin Small 'Bongo Jerry' – Jamaica, January 2008

Mr Andrew Bryan – Northampton, March 2008

Mrs Jackie Edwards – London, April 2008

This highly visible force is influential internationally in music (reggae), food, fashion (dreadlocks), dance and language. In view of this, I will seek to highlight the Rastafarian Movement by explaining its origin, beliefs, culture and its influence from a global point of view, as well as when and why it came to Britain and what created its prevalence.

Rastafarianism may be seen as a new religious movement that has arisen from Judaism and Christianity. The Oxford English Dictionary defines Rastafarianism as "religious movement in the Caribbean mainly among people of Jamaican origin",[2] holding that Emperor Haile Selassie I of Ethiopia was the Messiah and that 'black' people are the chosen people. With respect to those beliefs, Rastafarianism is not an organized religion; instead, it is a movement and an ideology. Many Rastas say that it is not a "religion" at all, but a rather a "Way of Life".[3] The Rastafari movement was born in Jamaica in the 1930s after Selassie's coronation in Ethiopia. Followers started to worship Selassie I, who died in 1975, as a type of Messiah, in the light of a 1920 prophecy by Jamaican civil rights leader Marcus Garvey that a Black man would be crowned king in Africa.

History

The Rastafarian movement began with the teachings, and parting words, of Marcus Mosiah Garvey (1887-1940) as he left Jamaica to settle in Harlem, New York. Garvey was a self-educated and well-educated man, the "exalted chief architect" who helped to mastermind, engineer and stimulate the mental and social environment of his country.[4] Garvey's political and cultural vision helped to inspire Leonard Howell to develop the foundations of this world view. The Black Jamaican foretold that there would be a Black Messiah in Africa –"Haile Selassie I, the former Emperor of Ethiopia, as the incarnation of God, called Jah".[5]

Garvey taught that Africans are the true Israelites and have been exiled to Jamaica and other parts of the world as divine punishment. He encouraged pride in being Black and worked to reverse the mindset of inferiority that centuries of enslavement had ingrained on the minds of Blacks. Garvey is regarded as a second John the Baptist, and famously prophesied in 1927: "Look to Africa, for there a king shall be crowned".[6]

Without doubt, Garvey was a man with many philosophies and opinions, and some of his messages were of unity and stated that all should be treated equally. This included freedom, education, job prospects and political and social status. In one of Garvey's Declaration of Rights, he states, "We protest against segregated districts, separate public conveyances, industrial discrimination, lynching and limitations of political privileges of any Negro citizen in any part of the world on account of race, colour or creed, and will exert our full influence and power against all such."[7] Yet, as a man that is regarded as John the Baptist, it is clear that in his forty 'Declaration Rights' he speaks of only one race, the Negro. He preaches segregation from the 'white' race, and that biracial or near-white communities should form their own race as they are neither Black nor White.[8]

Though Garvey spearheaded the movement with his strong beliefs in the slogan "Africa for Africans", there were a host of other significant and trail-blazing pioneers who operated within the cultural construct where Rastafarians originated.[9] Some of the earlier pioneers include John B. Russwurm, who in 1826 co-founded the *Freedom's Journal* in New York; Albert Thorne, a Barbadian born in 1860, who was an advocate of the 'Back to Africa' Movement; and Arthur Barclay, who was the 14th President of Liberia, serving from November 4, 1904 until January 1, 1912.[11] Arthur had migrated to Liberia along with several hundred other Caribbean people as early as 1865. Forgotten founders of the religion such as Leonard Howell came into conflict with the entire establishment in Jamaica, including the planters, the trade unions, established churches, police and colonial authorities. Nevertheless, this movement prospered, and today the Rastafari faith exists worldwide.[10]

Within the relatively brief life of the Rastafarian Movement, several prominent and active organizations have developed, which have served as pillars and supporters of the movement. The three main ones include: Nyahbinghi; Ethiopia-Africa Black International Congress (E.A.B.I.C.) or Bobo Shanti; and the Twelve Tribes of Israel.

The Bobo Shanti movement was founded in 1958 in Jamaica, by Prince Emmanuel Charles Edwards, considered by many to be the Black Christ. Prince Emmanuel, Marcus Garvey and Haile Selassie are regarded as part of a Holy Trinity. Selassie is regarded as King or God, Garvey is perceived to be a prophet, and Emmanuel a High Priest. The group can now be found in the Bahamas, Virgin Islands, Ghana, Nigeria, Ethiopia and Trinidad. Bobo Shanti wear brightly coloured turbans and long flowing robes, and women in Bobo Shanti must cover their arms and legs. The Bobo Shanti members live apart from society and their current base is in Bull Bay, Jamaica. They do not accept the laws and principles of Jamaican society.[11]

Nyahbinghi is the oldest of all the Rastafarian subgroups. Nyahbinghi attempts to keep the link between Rastafarian faith and African heritage close. The group is named after Queen Nyahbinghi who ruled Uganda in the nineteenth century and helped reduce the influence of colonial powers. The name Nyahbinghi is believed to mean 'Death to all Oppressors'. The focus of this group is on the veneration of Haile Selassie, who is regarded by them as the embodiment of God. Ethiopia is very important to the sect, who emphasise the repatriation of Blacks.[12]

The Twelve Tribes of Israel is a group founded in 1968. Vernon Carrington was its founder. He believed that it was his mission to reunite the Lost Tribes of Israel and he also claimed that everyone can be saved.

Ideology/Religious Beliefs

Rastafarians accept and recognize His Imperial Majesty Emperor Haile Selassie I, Jah Rastafari, born Lidj Tafari Makonnen, of Ethiopia (1892-1975) as the Supreme Father of Humanity and his Empress, Menen, as the Mother of Humanity. Although some Rastafarians still regard Haile Selassie I as Christ, the Black Messiah whose promised return or 'second coming' the Emperor fulfils, many modern adherents do not see this as central to their faith. Selassie is also seen as a living descendant of King Solomon and the King of Kings, Lord of Lords. As a result of their history of slavery and oppression, Rastas liken the fate of all Black people in the West to that of the Israelites, who were enslaved in Egypt and Babylon. They believe that they will not be free until they return to Africa. For many Rastas, Africa is a spiritual state rather than a geographical place. They do not believe in an afterlife, so Africa, and specifically Ethiopia, is seen as heaven on Earth, and is often called Zion.[13]

Worship for the Rastafarians is really the paying of homage or service to the Creator. This is not merely reserved for ceremonial occasions, but is an integral part of the day-to-day life or 'livity' of the Rastafarians. There are no intermediaries within Rastafarianism. Since the faith is an inborn concept, Rastafarians generally cultivate a personal relationship with The Most High, Jah Rastafari. However, it is interesting to note that the Ethiopia Africa Black International Congress- popularly referred to as Bobo Shanti - invokes the name of their congress leader, Prince Immanuel, in their prayers.[14]

Rastafarians' concept has diversified from its formation in Jamaica, West Indies in the 1930s. To make a comparison, western Christianity started in

Rome but today has thousands of different denominations, yet the image of Christ remains the central focus. Rastafarians have followed a similar pattern with the numerous splinter groups, yet His Imperial Majesty Emperor Haile Selassie I remains the central focal point. What cannot be denied is the fact that Rastafarianism, like Christianity, has brought about positive thinking and confidence for a great number of Black people worldwide, who would otherwise never have challenged the status quo.

Culture and Symbols

Rastafarians often wear items of clothing with the black, green, red, and yellow or gold stripes of the Ethiopian flag. The black represents nothing - that which was before the beginning - and everything. Red represents the blood of Africans and the foundation of all humanity. Blood means life, therefore Rastas do not willingly shed or eat blood. Green represents the land and vegetation of Africa, and by extension, the earth, and yellow represents the sun as a source of energy. It also represents the wealth of Africa, and the purity of light and life.

At present there are many Jamaicans who are Rastafarians, many of whom also take literally a biblical verse in the book Judges 13:2-5 which instructs against taking a razor to one's head.[15] The wearing of the dreadlocks is a living functional symbol and covenant of their devotion to the Most High.[16] Although many tend to believe that one needs to be clad with the 'locks', not everyone in the movement shares the same view. Many of the followers who themselves are Rastas state that "yuh don't haffi dread to be Rasta", which translates as: "you do not have to dread to be a Rasta".[17]

Marijuana has long been used to alleviate complaints such as high blood pressure, arthritis and chronic pains, to name a few. It can be eaten, prepared hot or cold as tea, or smoked if preferred, and Rastas use it as a part of the meditation process.[18] The ganja or marijuana (herb leaf) is a symbol of the medicinal and sacred properties and nature of herbs. According to Ixudah, "... ganja is a cultural healing herb and is an important gift from Jah". He also found that authors of the 1999 Institute of Medicine (IOM) report, 'Marijuana as Medicine', in assessing the science base, describe three types of pain that may be improved by cannabinoid, namely somatic pain, visceral pain, and neuropathic pain.[19] Researchers appear most interested in examining cannabis' ability to relieve neuropathic pain, which results from injury to nerves, peripheral receptors, or the central nervous system, because it is often

beliefs have been modified. Some the earlier Rasta beliefs included hatred of Whites, belief in the superiority of Blacks, faith that Blacks are God's chosen people, desire for revenge on Whites for their wickedness, and acknowledgement of Emperor Haile Selassie as God, and the ruler of Black people. Although some of these views and some beliefs remained unchanged for many Rastafarians, others arrived at different conclusions after Haile Selassie's remains were found in 1992.[30]

From the 1930s until the mid 1970s, most Rastafarians accepted the traditional Rastafari beliefs, and the idea of Babylon held by the Rastafarians has developed to represent all oppressive organisations (slave trade) and countries in the world. The basic tenets of early Rastafari, according to many leaders such as preachers Leonard Howell and Marcus Garvey, included some very strong statements about racial issues. This might be expected in the religion of an oppressed people living in exile. Fortunately, the previous Rastafarian belief that all White people are evil has diminished, and is no longer central to Rastafarian belief systems.

For most modern Rastafarians, the most important doctrine is not the belief in the divinity of Haile Selassie I. Some early Rastafarians, for example Bob Marley and other reggae singers, still regard Haile Selassie as the Black Messiah, but many modern adherents do not see this as being central to their beliefs. Instead, they choose to emphasise that Rastafarians are the chosen people of God and are on earth to promote his power and peacefulness.[31] Bob Marley and other modern Rastafarians have been providing the world with an insight into the changes in the group's beliefs. Thus, the ability to see clearly and intuitively into the nature of a complex religion such as Rastafarianism is being gradually achieved.

The evidence shows that the harsh reality of the slave trade for many Rastafarians, especially the contemporary ones, will always be fiercely resented: the fact that they were driven from the 'mainland' to the islands of the Caribbean and other parts of the world was against their will. It is clear that research has provided some evidence that there are differences between the early and modern ideologies of the complex Rastafarian Movement. Rastafarians differ in some of their doctrine but nonetheless, they all have one ultimate goal, which is to go back to Africa.

Finally, will those Rastafarians who are still concerned with the fulfilling of Marcus Garvey's 'Back to Africa' campaign continue their fight in order to reunite Africans with their 'Motherland' by abandoning contact with Western society? Where is that 'Motherland'? And why is it that the government of that 'Motherland' does not claim its people instead of leaving them in 'Hell' for so many years? Without a doubt, it is my belief that those who are still stuck in limbo should spend the precious time given from God to learn to forgive and, as hard as it may be, to forgive their oppressors. If Liberia or Ethiopia calls, then by all means answer; but until then, lives should be lived and enjoyed.

1 Y. Tafari, *Overstanding Rastafari. Jamaica's Gift to the World* (Jamaica: Senya-Cum, 2007), p.20.

2 *Concise Oxford English Dictionary* (Oxford: OUP, 2001), p.1188.

3 'Haile Selassie', Wikipedia, **http://en.wikipedia.org/wiki/Haile_Selassie_I_of_Ethiopia** (accessed 1 April, 2009).

4 Tafari, *Overstanding Rastafari*.

5 'Haile Selasssie'.

6 W. Zips (Ed.), *Rastafari* (Kingston: Ian Randle Publishers, 2006), p. 13-14.

7 A. Jacques- Garvey (Ed.), *A Philosophy and Opinion of Marcus Garvey* (New York: Athenaeum, 1977), p.138.

8 Jacques-Garvey, p.1.

9 Zips, p.3.

10 'Haile Selassie'.

11 BBC, 'Religion and Ethics – Rastafari', **http://www.bbc.co.uk/religions/religions/rastafari/subdivisions** (accessed 22 March, 2009).

12 BBC, 'Rastafari'.

13 Tafari, *Overstanding Rastafari*.

14 'Haile Selassie'.

15 *The Holy Bible* (London: Trinitarian Bible Society, 1958 ed.), p.314.

16 'Rasta Miss World?', *The Age* (on-line), **http//theage.com.au/ffximage/2007/05/21/300x358 rasta.jpg** (accessed 13 April, 2009).

17 M. Heritage, 'Don't haffi dread' (1999), **http://www.rastafarian.net** (accessed 13 April, 2009).

18 Information from A. Kowalska questionnaire, 'Personal beliefs and Practices as a Rastafarian' (completed by 6 respondents in Jamaica and Britain, 2009).

19 Ixudah, 'Your email from around the world' (2007), **http://www.rastafarian.net** (accessed 13 April, 2009).

20 Kowalska questionnaire, 2009.

21 'Rasta Miss World?'.

22 L.Latzko, 'Traditional Rastafarian Food' (2009), **http://www.ehow.co.uk/about 5103326 traditional-rastafarian-food.html?cr=1** (accessed 22 March 2009).

23 D.Wall, 'Green World: I am a Rasta. I am also an MP for the Green Party' (2003), **http://another-green-world.blogspot.com/2006/04/i-am-rasta-i-am-also-mp-for-green.html** (accessed 22 March 2009).

24 P. Byron, 'Japanese Rasta' (2009), **http://www.flickr.com/photos/petermbyron/3515252160** (accessed 22 March 2009).

25 N. Redington, 'A Sketch of Rastafarian History', **http://www.nomadfx.com/old/rasta1.html** (accessed 22 March 2009).

26 B. Chevannes, *Rastafari: Roots and Ideology* (New York: Syracuse University Press, 1994), p.104.

27 B. Marley, 'Buffalo Soldier' (1983).

28 Chevannes, *Rastafari*.

29 A. Kowalska, anonymous male interviewee, 'Personal Beliefs and Practices', University of Northampton, 2009.

30 BBC, 'Haile Selassie laid to Rest', **http://news.bbc.co.uk/1/hi/world/africa/1007736.stm** (accessed 2 April 2009).

31 J. Owens, *The Rastafarians of Jamaica* (Kingston: Sangsters Book Store, 1976).

Bibliography

Chevannes, B., *Rastafari: Roots and Ideology*
(New York: Syracuse University Press, 1994)

The Holy Bible (London: Trinitarian Bible Society, 1958 ed.)

Jacques-Garvey, A. (ed.), *A Philosophy and Opinion of Marcus Garvey*
(New York: Athenaeum, 1977)

Owens, J., The Rastafarians of Jamaica
(Kingston: Sangsters Book Store, 1976)

Tafari, Y., *Overstanding Rastafari. Jamaica's Gift to the World*
(Jamaica: Senya-Cum, 2007)

Zips, W. (ed.), *Rastafari* (Kingston: Ian Randle Publishers, 2006)

Kowalska, A., 'Personal beliefs and Practices as a Rastafarian',
questionnaires and interviews with six anonymous respondents in Britain
and Jamaica, 2009

The Age (online), (accessed 13 April 2009),
http//theage.com.au/ffximage/2007/05/21/300x358 rasta.jpg

'Haile Selassie', Wikipedia (accessed 1 April 2009),
http://en.wikipedia.org/wiki/Haile_Selassie_I_of_Ethiopia

Other websites:

http://www.rastafarian.net (accessed 13 April, 2009)

http://www.ehow.co.uk/about 5103326 traditional-rastafarian-food.html?cr=1
(accessed 22 March 2009)

http://another-green-world.blogspot.com/2006/04/i-am-rasta-i-am-also-mp-for-green.html
(accessed 22 March 2009)

http://www.flickr.com/photos/petermbyron/3515252160
(accessed 22 March 2009)

http://www.nomadfx.com/old/rasta1.html
(accessed 22 March 2009)

http://news.bbc.co.uk/1/hi/world/africa/1007736.stm
(accessed 2 April 2009)

Chapter 10

Caribbean Food from Past to Present

by Shirley Brownbill

For many years I have had a great interest in food, and the opportunity to research Caribbean food from past to present was a topic that I was eager to undertake. Firstly, I will explore how history has shaped what we eat. Secondly I will show some of the influences that have impacted on Caribbean foods past and present. It has to be noted that historically countries such as Africa, India, America, Spain and Europe have had strong influences on Caribbean food. Americans brought maize and cassava, Africans brought garden plants, such as okra and ackee, domesticated pigs and cattle came from Europe, and citrus fruit and rice from Asia.

In order to demonstrate how different countries contributed to Caribbean food, I will look at slavery establishing what and where slaves ate, what slave masters allowed them to eat, and what they did to supplement their diet. In addition to this I will explore what was classed as a special meal for the slaves. When looking at utensils, there is a kitchen utensil called the coal pot which is a historical kitchen item. I will explain how this has survived slave times and has now become known as a Dutch pot. When concluding my study I will reflect on how food and diet have changed, especially over the last fifty years in Britain, for African Caribbean people.

As a Black British Caribbean woman, I have noted that over the years food has played an important part in my family life. Within Caribbean culture, at functions such as weddings, christenings, birthdays and funerals food plays a major role. In particular cake plays an important part, as this is usually the centre piece of any event. As time has gone by the cakes have become more and more elaborate, which can possibly be associated with status within the community. I am from Jamaican parentage and my study will reflect this. The Caribbean is made up of many different islands and although there are some overlaps each island has its own individual culture. While food plays in important role in many other cultures, the purpose of this chapter is to focus on the historical context of Caribbean food from past to present.

In undertaking my research, I have used the following methods and sources: my own personal experience and love of food; books; internet; interviews with three elders from different Caribbean Islands; oral history testimony; and a visit to the Natural History Museum. The reasons for me using a range of methods and sources was to support what I have learnt over the years and to find out how history has impacted on Caribbean food over the years.

The Early Years

The Arawak, Carib and Taino Indians were the first inhabitants of the Caribbean Islands. Their daily diet consisted of vegetables and fruits such as papaw, yams, guavas, and cassava. The Taino started the process of cooking meat and fish in large clay pots. It has been stated by many historians that the Arawak Indians were the first people of Jamaica. It has been said that the Arawaks were very peaceful people and lived in the villages near the coast. Their principal foods were cassava, corn, sweet potatoes, pimento, fish guavas, and pineapple. The Arawaks devised a method of slow-cooking meat over flavoured wood. This grate was called a barbacoa, and the word we know today as barbeque is taken from this early Indian cooking method. The Africans that were brought to Jamaica came from a number of different tribes and the most dominant appeared to have been the Ashanti and Fanti peoples, and then the Yoruba and Ibo people.[1]

In 1492 Christopher Columbus discovered Jamaica, but it was not until the early sixteenth century that permanent settlers were finally established. As Columbus was under the rule of Spain, Spanish products such as the banana, plantain, lemon, lime, coconut, pomegranate and grapes were imported to the island. The Spanish learned from the Indians the methods of preserving meat and fish by smoking; they then introduced frying which is still very common in Jamaica and in England today. For the Caribbean elders in England, frying or 'browning' as they say is still very common.

Food and African Slavery

When the Europeans brought African slaves to the Caribbean, the slave diet consisted mostly of food the slave owners did not want to eat. So slaves had to be inventive; they blended their traditional African foods with staple foods found on the islands. The Africans introduced okra, also known as lady's finger, callaloo from the spinach family, fish cakes, salt fish, ackee, mangoes, pudding and souse, as well as other items.[2] Slaves were divided into two categories: house slaves and field slaves. The house slaves usually had better food than the field slaves.

Slaves were given salted beef, pork and fish by their masters once a year. As a result of this, slaves became accustomed to the taste and this food choice has been passed down from generation to generation. Slaves prepared their food rations using simple cooking techniques taken from the African homelands or from the native Indians. This has had a major impact on health issues for Caribbean people, as the high salt diet has been linked to high blood pressure and diabetes.

Although food stuffs were usually distributed to slaves for cooking, a main meal was sometimes served from a central kitchen. Slaves prepared their meals on an open fire by roasting and boiling. Jerome Handler and F.W. Lange suggest that meals were nutritious and monotonous, and that food allowances were often small amounts. This resulted in slaves stealing food from their masters.[3] Kiple stated that it was not considered wrong to steal food from their masters, but knowing how slaves were treated, I personally believe that this could not always have been the case. Slaves had to grow their own food to supplement the little food their slave masters gave them. They were given a certain amount of ground on which to grow their own provisions and this land was referred to as 'Negro Land'. They grew things such as yam, pigeon peas, okra, callaloo, corn, cocoa and coffee.

As a woman within the slave master's house, if you were 'favoured' through having a sexual relationship you were given extra food provisions and some rum. This would be then shared with family members and other slaves within that household. Slave markets developed in Jamaica as slaves grew more and more provisions, and Amelioration Laws issued in the British Antilles encouraged other islands to grow their own provisions. As a result of this, slaves who produced their own foods ate better diets. The Europeans were concerned that the slaves should not develop a taste for fresh meat as it would have financial implications for the masters if slaves were supplied with fresh meat. For a while slaves were prohibited from rearing cattle.

As food supplements were minimal, the most popular method of cooking for the slaves was in a large cast-iron pot. This was referred to as a coal pot and all the ingredients that were available to the slaves were put into the pot and cooked. For slaves, due to the much oppressed conditions they had to live in, special meals were far and few between. At Christmas they did the best they could with the excess crops that they grew and sold at the market: they were then able to have a special Christmas meal. Also, weddings were seen as a special occasion for slaves to use any so-called luxury provisions they had. Sometimes they would have a little rum that might have been given to the 'favoured' female. A 'cook up' is an example of a traditional dish cooked for holidays and festive occasions. This was cooked in a coal pot and consisted of all the seasonal vegetables that slaves had access to. If they were lucky the 'cook up' might have some meat in it. The 'cook up' has many variations in different Caribbean Islands and is still very popular when friends and family get together.[4] These special meals could be very short-lived as slaves could be sold without prior notice.

Some Historic Traditions

I stated earlier that the coal pot has a historic place in the Caribbean kitchen: it has survived over the years with a modern slant. The coal pot is a pot that the slaves used on a daily basis. This pot was always on the grate or fire with something in it to feed the slaves. Over the years the coal pot has evolved into what is now called the Dutch pot, and the majority of Caribbean homes have a Dutch pot which is an oval shape and starts its life a bright silver colour. With much use over the years, the pot becomes very dark and it is said by many owners that the darker the Dutch pot the better the food cooks. There was always a pot on the grate – as a child my Mum use to ask me to "turn the fire down under the pot." I never questioned this as I knew it meant I needed to turn down the gas gauge on the cooker. I discussed this with my Mum one day, and she explained that this expression has been passed down since slavery times when the pot was literally on the fire.

Some traditional meals that have been passed on through the Caribbean have a historical context and are still very prevalent now. Though my research has focussed on food, it has to be acknowledged that music, religion and health have also influenced food practices. An example of this is in the times of slavery the first yield of any crops was taken to the church to be blessed by the minister. I will now elaborate on three particular dishes that have a historic place in Caribbean cookery.

Journey cakes are also known as fried dumplings, fritters, bakes, hoecake, battercake and jonny cakes. The name journey cake is said to have derived

of reasons. One is the change in the family unit. With the demise of the extended family unit and with families not living in the same geographic area, sometimes it is difficult to buy West Indian food, and when the food is available it can be very expensive as the choice is very limited. This then impacts on the type of food that can be bought. This I know from personal experience, as I originally moved from South London to Wellingborough and due to the high cost of West Indian food here in Wellingborough I had to adjust my diet, resulting in what was a regular Caribbean meal being now treated as a luxury.

A second reason for the change in diet is the cultural diversity of families. Interracial relationships are one of the largest-growing family units in England, and with this change eating habits become more varied. For a family where the mother is European and the father is Black (in this context referring to someone who is Caribbean, African or Asian), the woman may not be able to cook the food that her partner is used to having. So their children may not experience the Black food on a regular basis.

Life-style also plays a major role. With people working long hours, food does not always play a major part in their lives. The advent of convenience foods and living in a throw-away culture means that home-made Caribbean food is slowing dying out. However, I have noticed recently that major supermarkets are now selling Caribbean meals for the microwave, showing how shops are diversifying to cater for the needs of Black and minority groups. It has to be noted that Black elders across Britain cook Caribbean food in the same way. I have been to Leeds, Derby, Birmingham, Wales and many other towns and cities visiting relatives, and they still cook the traditional dishes without any variations even though they live at opposite ends of the country.

Conclusion

Caribbean food is a melting pot of different cultures that have shaped the islands historically, including the cultures of Africa, India, China, Spain, Denmark, Portugal, France and Britain. It is no wonder Caribbean cooking is so rich and creative, with flavours of all these countries. In the Caribbean the food that is still served today has been influenced by the cultures of the world, but each island adds its own special flavour and cooking technique. Caribbean food has crossed the waters and stayed with us, even though some dishes have become Europeanised. We can see that Caribbean food past and present will stay with us for as long as individuals hold on to their culture, even though the diverse make-up of the family unit has changed and is still changing.

[1] N. Benghiat, *Traditional Jamaican Cooking* (London: Penguin,1985).

[2] L. Thompkins, 'Caribbean Food – A Little History', Ezine Articles (accessed 15 March 2007), **http://ezinearticles. com/?Caribbean-Food---A-Little-History&id=45781**

[3] F. Kiple and K. Ornelas Conee, *The Cambridge World History Of Food*, Vol. 2 (Cambridge: Cambridge University Press, 2000).

[4] C. Mackie, *Life and Food in the Caribbean* (Kingston: Ian Randle,1995).

[5] E. Donaldson, *The Real Taste Of Jamaica* (Kingston: Ian Randle,1994).

[6] F. Dowe, M. Dalrymple and Y. Field, *The Caribbean Black Cake* (London:Youth A.I.D. Lewisham, 1999).

[7] M. Phillips and T. Phillips, *Windrush: the Irresistible Rise of Multicultural Britain* (London: Harper Collins,1998).

Bibliography

Benghiat, N., *Traditional Jamaican Cooking* (London: Penguin, 1985)

Donaldson, E., *The Real Taste Of Jamaica* (Kingston: Ian Randle, 1994)

Dowe, F., M. Dalrymple and Y. Field, *The Caribbean Black Cake* (London:Youth A.I.D. Lewisham, 1999)

Kiple, F. and K. Ornelas Conee, *The Cambridge World History Of Food*, Vol. 2 (Cambridge: Cambridge University Press, 2000)

Mackie, C., *Life and Food in the Caribbean* (Kingston: Ian Randle, 1995)

Phillips, M. and Trevor Phillips, *Windrush: the Irresistible Rise of Multicultural Britain* (London: Harper Collins,1998)

On-line sources

Thompkins, L., 'Caribbean Food – A Little History', Ezine Articles (accessed 15 March 2007)

http://ezinearticles.com/?Caribbean-Food---A-Little-History&id=45781

Wikepedia, 'Cornbread' (accessed 24 March 2007)
http://en.wikipedia.org/wiki/Cornbread

Chapter 11

Sake Dean Mahomed

by Heather Knighton

The life of Sake Dean Mahomed is an important story. As a young soldier he was part of the East India Company, and so essentially part of the British Empire. After losing his father he decided to pursue a new life in Britain. In the years that followed he managed to become a recognised entrepreneur in business. Another notable achievement was his literary success. He became the first Indian author to write his books in English. How much of his incredible life story is known? I am going to look at Sake Dean Mahomed's life and assess whether his achievements were entirely successful. Did he adapt his beliefs in order to accustom himself to his new life in Britain? Did he use his 'Indian charm' to propagate his reputation as a respected businessman?

Early Life in India, Ireland and London

Sake Dean Mahomed was born in Patna, India, in 1759. His father was an Indian officer in the East India Company Company's army, which was stationed in Bengal. Mahomed received a traditional Islamic education, and both his parents were practising Shi'ite Muslims.

Mahomed's father was killed during a battle against recalcitrant landowners, which spurred him into following in his father's footsteps. He joined as a camp follower to Ensign Godfrey Evan Baker of the 3rd European Regiment. During this time the French colonisers of India were defeated. Mahomed had a successful career in the army. He was active in several battles, notably helping to quash the resistance of those opposed to British rule in the Benares region. He had become a close friend of Baker, and when Baker resigned from his position of Captain, after allegedly extorting money from villagers, Mahomed decided to follow him. Britain had by this time established itself as the foremost power of the globe with a formidable naval strength. Muslims of the time were encouraged to work as lascars on British ships.

taking over as head of the business. During the Victorian period the novelty of Indian baths and the demand for Mahomed's services began to subside. In December 1850 Mahomed's wife died of cancer, and Mahomed himself died of "natural decay" two months later.

Mahomed and his beloved wide are buried together at St Nicholas's Parish Church in Brighton. His death came three months before the opening of the Great Exhibition of 1851, which symbolised the strength of the British Empire. This exhibition should perhaps have included his innovative bath houses, which had been so highly sought after by the elite.

Sake Dean Mahomed was an interesting man who achieved considerable success in Britain through his determined ability as an entrepreneur. This was evident throughout his life, even when his plans were not necessarily successful. For an Indian migrant to come to England and become appointed as the King's Shampooing Surgeon was an achievement which highlights his rugged determination to make a positive impact on British society.[6] Not only was Mahomed successful in pioneering his own restaurant and shampooing baths: he was also one of the first Indians to have his works published in English. His prominence is clearly revealed by the fact that he had 320 elite British subscribers to his book. He was recognised as a 'man of letters' in literary circles even at an early stage of his career.[7]

Image and Reputation

Mahomed's ethnicity played a role in his entrepreneurship. He was seen in a positive light by the elite due to his customs and culture, which he practised while it was seen to be advantageous to the prosperity of his business. Throughout the sixty years he lived in Britain, he continuously re-imaged his appearance in order to distinguish himself from the stereotypes of other Indian figures. When he was appointed by King George IV, he had an official court costume made which was modelled on Mughal imperial court dress. This added to his exoticism. Mahomed used his Indian presence when it was seen to be advantageous to his popularity as an expert in the field of Indian treatments. Giving himself a strong self-identification as a native of India helped to qualify him as a "master of eastern knowledge".[8]

Mahomed did not have an easy transition into British society. He received hostile criticisms of his work. His son Horatio wrote that there was "tremendous opposition: the public press teemed with abuse, the medical faculty shook their heads and doubted...ninety-nine in a hundred of the public at large" considered his cure to be nothing more than "a cheat and a Hindoo juggle".[9] Mahomed overcame this hurdle by offering free treatments to show the public that his techniques were revolutionary in the treatment of ailments through the use of herbal remedies. Some clients who had undergone treatment at other institutions were given free treatments by Mahomed. This resulted in several cures, arousing interest and bringing in an expanding client base. Mahomed's book *Cases Cured* was another catalyst, creating a new wave of clients. He was very aware of the importance of advertising his services and knew that his book provided a 'guarantee' that his treatments worked.

Mahomed was raised in India as a Muslim yet when he married his wife in Ireland they were married in an Anglican church, accepting the faith of the Church of England. It is not evident whether Mahomed fully embraced this faith or whether he did so in order to become accepted into British society. It could be suggested that he did accept the faith: one of his grandsons, Reverend James Kerriman Mahomed, was to be appointed as a Vicar of Hove in Sussex. [10] This fact highlights the degree to which his descendants eventually integrated into Christian English society. Mahomed also named all his children with popular English names: none of them had Muslim names.

The logistics of the time could be seen as attributing to his success, as Brighton during this period was a town that was developing into a fashionable resort for the health-conscious. The population of Brighton expanded from 2,000 in 1750 to 4,000 in 1780 and over 7,000 in 1801, reaching 65,000 by 1850. One of the main reasons for growth was the introduction of the railway, enabling people to travel easily to Brighton for holidays or business. Dr Richards Russell's work on the use of the properties of sea water within the health sphere also contributed to the large numbers flocking towards the coasts.

Historical Legacies

Pakistani literary critic Muneeza Shamsie suggests that Sake Dean Mahomed began to lose his prominence during the Victorian period and was forgotten about until the 1970s and 1980s, when the poet and scholar Alamgir Hashmir focused new attention on his work. Further interest has been generated by Michael Fisher's biography. Some of Mahomed's legacy is nowadays recognised. The site in Portman Place where he first opened his Hindoostanee coffee shop has been awarded one of the green plaques awarded to celebrate the lives of distinguished residents of Westminster. Yet his books are very hard to find. I could not obtain a single copy of any of his works within the library system connected to the University of Northampton, nor through the public library system. Information needs to be made much more easily available in order to ensure that future generations can be educated about the lives of those who were migrants to Britain. At present, more information is available to the general public on the internet than anywhere else.

I visited Brighton to see how the town has chosen to commemorate Sake Dean Mahomed. First I visited the hotel where his bath houses once stood. This site is now home to the Queen's Hotel. I was disappointed to find that the hotel did not have a plaque or any other form of acknowledgement to the bath houses, nor to the entrepreneur who created so much interest in the area with his iconic innovations for the town.

I next visited St Nicholas's Church in Dyke Road, Brighton, to see the final resting place of Sake Dean Mahomed. I walked around the grave yard and discovered several graves included in a heritage trail to highlight people buried there and their importance to Brighton's history. Sake Dean Mahomed was not among the select few included. In fact I could not find his grave at all. I thought this might be due to deterioration caused by the weather, as some gravestones no longer had visible inscriptions.[12] I believe that Sake Dean Mahomed should have been included in the heritage trail as he was an Indian migrant who embraced British culture. He made a big impact on the history of Brighton.

At the Brighton Pavilion a play was staged in April 2009 which, amongst other notable people, depicted the life of Sake Dean Mahomed. This was one positive way in which Brighton was keeping the story of Mahomed alive for the people of today. The Brighton and Hove Black History Association is another tool which has promoted interest in local Black and Asian history, encouraging those who visit the website to select a variety of people and themes.[13] A page of information is dedicated to the achievements of Sake Dean Mahomed. The Brighton and Hove Library also has several pages which give information about Sake Dean Mahomed's life, with pictures of his bath house and of Mahomed himself. The Brighton Museum also covers his life, and was a good base from which to start my research into his prolific local career.[14] Sake Dean Mahomed's court dress is on display at the Royal Pavilion, and features on the BBC website as part of the 2010 BBC project about the world's history in one hundred objects.[15]

After studying the life of Sake Dean Mahomed, I realise how important his story is in today's society. Britain is such a multicultural place which should have the history available to represent those cultures. Mahomed was definitely a positive figure from India. His books and pictures illustrate life for an ambitious Indian within the old British Empire. He provides an example of how people who have migrated from other countries could be accepted into British society.

1 H. Ansari, *The Infidel Within. Muslims in Britain Since 1800* (London: Hurst, 2004).

2 R. Visram, *Asians in Britain. 400 Years of History* (London: Pluto Press, 2002).

3 **http://www.fathom.com/course/21701766/ sessions5.html** (accessed 20 April 2009).

4 **http://www.victorianturkishbath. org/2HISTORY/AtoZHist/HotAir/pix/ Mahomed w.htm** (accessed 20 May 2009).

5 **http://www.victorianturkishbath. org/2HISTORY/AtoZ/HotAir/pix/ Mahomed w.htm** (accessed 20 May 2009).

6 National Archives, *Moving Here,* **http://www.movinghere.org.uk/galleries/ roots/asian/tracingasianroots/dean_ma homed3.htm#** (accessed 20 April 2009).

7 Oxford Dictionary of National Biography, **www.oxforddnb.com/articles/53/53351- article.html?back** (accessed 19 January 2009).

8 A. Kumar, *The Indian Writer an Expatriate* (London: Routledge, 2004).

9 Visram, p.41.

10 **http://www.absoluteastronomy.com/topics/ Sake_Dean_Mahomet** (accessed 20 April 2009).

11 R. Fisher, *The First Indian Author in English: Dean Mahomed (1759-1851) in India, Ireland and England* (Oxford: Oxford University Press, 1996).

12 Brighton and Hove Black History have since confirmed the location of his grave within this churchyard.

13 Brighton and Hove Black History, **www.black-history.org.uk.**

14 Brighton History Centre, **www.brighton-hove-rpml.org.uk.**

15 Royal Pavilion, **www.royalpavilion.org.uk**; BBC website, 'A History of the World in 100 objects', **www.bbc.co.uk/ahistoryoftheworld.**

Bibliography

Ansari, H., *The Infidel Within. Muslims in Britain Since 1800*
(London: Hurst, 2004)

Fisher, M., *The First Indian Author in English: Dean Mahomed* (1759-1851)
in India, Ireland and England (Oxford: Oxford University Press, 1996)

Kumar, A. A., *The Indian Writer an Expatriate* (London: Routledge, 2004)

Oxford Dictionary of National Biography
(Oxford: Oxford University Press, 2004)

Visram, R., *Asians in Britain. 400 Years of History*
(London: Pluto Press, 2002)

Websites:

http://www.fathom.com/course/21701766/sessions5.htmlhttp://www.
victorianturkishbath.org/2HISTORY/AtoZHist/HotAir/pix/Mahomed w.htm

http://www.movinghere.org.uk/galleries/roots/asian/tracingasianroots/dean_
mahomed3.htm#

www.oxforddnb.com/articles/53/53351-article.html?back

http://www.absoluteastronomy.com/topics/Sake_Dean_Mahomet

www.black-history.org.uk

www.brighton-hove-rpml.org.uk

www.royalpavilion.org.uk

www.bbc.co.uk/ahistoryoftheworld

this the East India Company stepped in and began to build accommodation for the Lascars, and by 1795 the Company had erected rock-bottom lodgings in the worst parts of London and other seafaring cities. When members of the Asiatic Society (established 1814) visited these accommodations they found that Lascars were sleeping on bare boards with little or no blankets in unheated buildings, and they were being flogged repeatedly. Even this minimal accommodation was soon to vanish with the decline of the East India Company, which was theoretically responsible under the Lascar Act of 1832 for the accommodation and care of the Lascars. Once again they were cast on to the streets to find their own accommodation, where they were introduced to gambling and the underworld of London.

Philanthropists realised that they had to intervene and from 1857, with donations from India-enriched merchants and Indian princes, the Strangers' Home for Asiatics was opened in London. It clothed, fed, sheltered and rehabilitated stray Lascars. This was to carry on until the beginning of the Great War.

Lascar activism during World War I and World War II

As we know, the demand for Lascars was high. The start of World War I increased this demand to an even greater extent. In 1916, due to the high rates of Lascar demand, contracts were extended to eighteen months. In addition, lured by better wages and the prospect of a better life, many men jumped ship in Britain and others may have left to join other ships or on shore businesses offering better wages. The Liverpool Steam Ships Owners Association blamed the increase in Lascar desertions on organised attempts to lure them into "more remunerative employment" on shore, warning of serious consequences to shipping if they were unable to fill vacancies in war-time.[14] Companies such as Lever Brothers in Merseyside, who had hired a considerable amount of Lascars to work in their factories, appealed to the East India Company and the Board of Trade not to take their Indian workers away from them in these war-reduced times. Furthermore the Lascars who found themselves employed and settled in Britain often did not want to return to India when they were told they had to. They were earning more money than they ever had before, and they had established a home for themselves.

During the Second World War Indian seamen comprised 20 per cent of the British maritime labour force. They faced the same turmoil and hardship on ships as White British seamen, yet their conditions had barely improved whereas the White British seamen's had got better. The Second World War is where we see the conditions and treatment of Lascars really begin to change, after decades of racial discrimination. Facing the same risks in wartime as their British counterparts, Indian seamen refused to sail without a wage increase, basic provisions and security for their families. Within weeks riots had spread throughout London, Liverpool and Glasgow: "Their compliance could no longer be taken for granted."[15] This clearly shows how a picture of a harmonious united Britain was just a propaganda piece.

Only three days into war in September 1939, as many as eight ships were on strike. Indian seamen were demanding as much as a 200 per cent pay rise. They also wanted essential provisions such as soap, warm clothing and bedding, showing how ship-owners were neglecting their duties and not looking after their employees. As the government could not tolerate strikes at this crucial point in time, the Board of Trade was forced into negotiations. Even though they threatened Lascars with widespread unemployment, the Lascars would not budge. In September 1939 a mere 25 per cent rise in basic wages was announced, which was still lower than any British men, who were gaining an extra £3 a month as a 'war risk' bonus. This further emphasises how a White life was valued more.

Across the country, on different ships Lascars were standing up for their rights. For example the crew of the SS Oxfordshire refused to work until their wages were increased. The captain refused them food until they did so and the strike carried on for nine days until eventually one of the seamen died and the captain gave in and gave a 100 per cent wage increase. Soon pay rises were in effect around the country.

Eventually it was realised that there was a need for Lascar compliance and a central Seamen's Welfare Board in London was set up to make sure that they received sufficient care. Finally Lascar patriotism and services during the War were being recognised. A statement from the High Commissioner's Office was issued thanking the people of India for their services and bravery during these hard times. Lascars for the first time were being recognised and appreciated for their hard work and efforts. The average wage rose by five times the pre-war rate to 130 rupees a month (£6. 15s. to £9. 7s.), illustrating a very noticeable change in the treatment of Lascars.[16]

Conclusion

This chapter highlights only the main stepping stones and developments in the history of Lascars. They have such an amazing and varied history, dating back over 400 years, that it is very difficult to narrow it down.

Though this account stops at the end of the Second World War, Lascars continued giving their services for many years after. This was an appropriate place to stop my research as this is the point in time when Lascars' fortunes and conditions began to take a turn for the better and their skills as seamen were finally beginning to be recognised.

One must ask the question why it took so long for Lascars to be accepted and for their conditions to change. There are many answers to this question, but probably one of the most simple is the lack of understanding and ignorance shown by the British towards their fellow seamen. Lack of understanding about one another's cultures, religions and practices all sparked antagonisms and racism and the belief that a White life is worth more than a Black one. This treatment was present for many years, making it hard to understand why these highly skilled men would offer their services to the British. One can only suggest that a hope for a new life for themselves and their families spurred them on.

Lascars should never be forgotten in our British history. They helped make the East India Company great, even though they faced many hardships and tribulations along the way. They also helped tremendously towards our maritime war effort, but it is equally important that they are remembered for their courage and determination when confronted with racism and hostility.

"Those nameless thousands have no memorial; they are perished as though they have never been..."[17]

1 Visram, R., *Asians in Britain. 400 years of History* (London: Pluto Press, 2002), p.15.

2 Humayun, A., *The Infidel Within: The History of Muslims in Britain* (London: C.Hurst, 2004), p.35.

3 Fathom, 'The First Asians in Britain, The Demand for Lascar Labour' (accessed 5 March 2008), **www.fathom.com/course/21701766/session2.html**

4 Visram (2002), p.16.

5 C. Adams, *Across Seven Seas and Thirteen Rivers* (London: THAP Books, 1987), p.16.

6 Adams, p. 17.

7 Fathom (accessed 5 March 2008).

8 Visram, R., *Ayahs, Lascars and Princes* (London: Pluto Press,1986), p.35.

9 M. Watkins-Thomas, 'Our Asian Crews' (accessed 25 February 2008), **www.Lascars.co.uk/crew.html.**

10 Adams, p.23.

11 Visram (2002), p.226.

12 Visram (2002), p.227.

13 Visram (1986), p.38.

14 Visram (2002), p.197.

15 Visram (2002), p.234.

16 Visram (2002), p.252.

17 Adams, p.209.

Bibliography

Adams, C., *Across Seven Seas and Thirteen Rivers. Life Stories of Pioneer Settlers in Britain* (London:THAP Books, 1987)

Ansari, H., *The Infidel Within: The History of Muslims in Britain, 1800 to the Present* (London: C Hurst, 2004)

Lahiri, S., *Indians in Britain. Anglo-Indian Encounters, Race and Identity, 1880-1930* (London: Frank Cass, 2000)

Visram, R., *Asians in Britain 400 Years of History* (London: Pluto Press, 2002)

Visram, R.,Ayahs, *Lascars and Princes* (London: Pluto Press, 1986)

Websites

British Library,'Asians in Britain: A Brief Outline (1600-1947)' (accessed 21 February 2008), **http://www.bl.uk/reshelp/findhelpsubject/history/history/asiansinbritain/histoutline/briefhist.html**

British Library,'Asians in Britain: Ayahs, Servants and Sailors' (accessed 21 February 2008),

http://www.bl.uk/reshelp/findhelpsubject/history/history/asiansinbritain/ayahsservantsandsailors/britishayahs.html

Fathom,'The First Asians in Britain, The Demand for Lascar Labour' (accessed 5 March 2008), **www.fathom.com/course/21701766/session2.html**

M. Watkins-Thomas,'Our Asian Crews' (accessed 25 February 2008), **www.lascars.co.uk/crew.html**

Chapter 13

Sophia Duleep Singh - Princess and Activist

by Jean Bouch

This is the story of Sophia Duleep Singh, Indian princess, Victorian socialite, political activist and unsung suffragette. In this study I have researched the family background, personal qualities, cultural heritage and political influences which led Sophia Duleep Singh to occupy her unique position in twentieth century women's history.

What were the qualities which enabled her to confront and overcome the prejudices and practices of Victorian England and make her stand for equality and women's rights? How did she combine her role as English lady with her position as Sikh princess and suffragette? Did she live a life in parallel, moving effortlessly between these different worlds, or did she face conflict and discrimination?

Using evidence from Princess Sophia's diaries, the Duleep Singh family papers, archives at the Women's Library, records at Hampton Court Palace, publications of the suffrage movement and other books and articles, I will try to answer these questions and to explore her connections with suffragettes and Indians in Britain, as well as her involvement with India itself.

Early Life and Influences

Born on 8 August 1876, Princess Sophia was the youngest daughter of Duleep Singh, deposed Maharaja of the Punjab and his young Egyptian wife, Maharani Bamba. Sophia enjoyed a country childhood with her five brothers and sisters at Elveden Hall, Norfolk, the Maharaja's country seat. This was a childhood befitting a member of the aristocracy, with dogs and ponies, shooting parties, grand balls and exotic social functions.[1] Maharaja Duleep Singh was renowned as a generous and lively host; his extravagances were legion. His parties were attended by aristocratic guests who were happy

As Diane Atkinson explains, "At the turn of the century the existing campaign for women's suffrage was organised by ladylike, low key and law abiding suffragists."[8] 1903 saw the dawn of a new era with the launch of the Women's Social and Political Union (WSPU). The WSPU chose a new, high-profile, daring and civilly disobedient approach.[9] They adopted militant tactics which challenged not only the legality of taxation without representation, but also society's deeply entrenched beliefs and values about the propriety, morality and equality of its women. Suffragettes were reviled as unwomanly and unsexed; they were brutally manhandled and abused as they made their protests.

It was to the WSPU and the Women's Tax Resistance League (WTRL) that Princess Sophia gave her loyalty and allegiance. From 1909 onwards Sophia was an active member of both these organisations, campaigning both locally and nationally for women's right to vote. She adopted a high-profile strategy of tax resistance and supported publicity campaigns with her very visible presence. She rode alongside Miss Shepherd in the Press Cart leading the publication day processions for 'Votes for Women'. She sold copies of *The Suffragette* at the gates of Hampton Court Palace, flaunting her protest at the very heart of the establishment. As a result of national and local suffragette violence, Hampton Court Palace, her place of residence, was closed for a total of six weeks in 1912 and again in 1913. Extra police were requested in 1913 because of the level of agitation.[10]

There was strong support for the suffragettes' cause in the area around Kew and Hampton Court. Princess Sophia was active in the Richmond and Kew and Kingston and District WSPU branches. She spoke regularly at meetings of the Richmond branch, and chaired meetings of the Kingston and District branch.[11] Testimony to the seriousness of her commitment and the extent of her contribution to the movement for women's suffrage is her presence in the deputation to Parliament on 'black Friday', 18 November 1910. More than four hundred women marched on Parliament. A deputation of twelve was selected to seek an audience with the Prime Minister. This deputation, headed by Mrs. Pankhurst, included Princess Sophia. *Votes for Women* magazine describes "a surging throng where twelve defenceless women, four over seventy years, were being buffeted, mobbed, forced back from a double line of police that protected a liberal government from being reminded of its own principles...Deserted by their police escort, the band of twelve defenceless women were at the mercy of the idle jostling crowd."[12]

In this instance Princess Sophia's royal status was no protection from the heckling mob. She did not receive preferential treatment because of her royal position. However this does not appear to have been the case regarding her activities with the Tax Resistance League. There is some evidence to suggest that, despite her strong personal commitment to the cause and her militant stand, Princess Sophia was treated more leniently in the courts than were some of her less aristocratic contemporaries. Princess Sophia was fined for non-payment of her eight dog licences whereas Miss Andrews of Ipswich was gaoled in the first division for non-payment of one dog licence. Official policy towards tax resisters was not consistent: some were pursued relentlessly while others were left alone.[13]

In May 1911 Mr. Leon Costello represented Princess Sophia at Spelthorne Petty Sessions where, undeterred by her first fine, she was again prosecuted for non- payment of licences for five dogs, a carriage and a manservant, and fined £5. A report in *Votes for Women* stated:"We understand that the refusal, briefly reported in last week's issue, of the Princess Sophia Duleep Singh to pay her taxes, has aroused great interest. Mr. Leon Costello said in court that the Princess took a very prominent part in the Women's Suffrage Movement, and that she desired to come forth in this way to make a protest against the great injustice of taxing women who had no voice in the matter."[14]

In July 1911 Princess Sophia had a seven-stone diamond ring impounded under Warrant of Distress, to be sold by auction at Ashford. Official invitation cards, to the design of 'At Home' cards of the day, were produced and distributed to suffrage supporters who were encouraged to attend in person:

"The Princess Sophia Duleep Singh's goods will be
sold for tax resistance.
Tues. July 5th at Hicks, Station Rd, Ashford.
Meeting held at auction room after sale at 4p.m.
Train Waterloo to Ashford 2.10p.m. 2s.6d return."[15]

Votes for Women on 28 July reported that the sale was very well attended. The ring was purchased for £10 by Mrs Jopling Rowe, a wealthy supporter, and promptly returned to Princess Sophia. At the sale the Princess was well supported by suffragists, including representatives from Rome and Chicago: "It was felt by all present that the Princess had done her utmost to impress an otherwise 'anti' neighbourhood with the cause."[16]

The significance of such a high-profile stand should not be underrated. Undeterred by the public distaste and the opprobrium heaped upon female protestors, Princess Sophia, now aged thirty-six, continued her militant activities. In December 1913 she appeared at Feltham Police Court charged with employing a manservant, keeping two dogs and a carriage without licence. It was here that she made her protest speech:

> I am unable conscientiously to pay money to the state, as I am not allowed to exercise any control over its expenditure; neither am I allowed any voice in choosing of Members of Parliament, whose salaries I have to help to pay. This is very unjust. When the women of England are enfranchised and the state acknowledges me as a citizen I shall, of course, pay my share willingly towards its upkeep. If I am not a fit person for the purpose of representation, why should I be a fit person for taxation?[17]

Her strong stand, albeit from a position of comfort and status, showed her willingness to jeopardise her position and acceptance among the upper-class elite in support of her beliefs and values. Variously described as firebrand, fanatical suffragette and passionate activist, Princess Sophia's commitment to the suffrage movement was never in doubt. The only Indian woman in the Tax Resistance League, she was visible, articulate and newsworthy.

The campaigning activities of the WSPU and Tax Resistance League ceased with the outbreak of war in 1914. Princess Sophia retained her connections with the suffragettes, remained loyal to the Pankhursts and supported the Suffragette Fellowship until her death in 1948. The strength of her loyalty and connection is evidenced by the fact that after Mrs Pankhurst's death in 1928, Sophia was appointed president of the committee responsible for providing flowers for her statue.

Princess Sophia and the Indian Connection

At the turn of the century, there were a number of students, politicians, revolutionaries, doctors, lawyers and royals who formed the Indian elite. These were the Indians in Britain with whom Princess Sophia would have had contact. In addition there were lascars, ayahs and domestic servants in whom Princess Sophia showed a charitable interest, continuing her father's financial support for the Lascars' Club (a refuge for Indian seamen in Britain).

Indians in Britain were welcomed as tokens of empire, but not as individuals in their own right. British officials deplored the attention lavished on the Indian royals by the upper classes and the society press: "Their wealth and splendour dazzled, their presence at official functions was part of the pomp and splendour of the empire."[18]

Did Princess Sophia bask in reflected exoticism? Did prevailing views of Indian women apply to her? The popular press, including the suffragette press, presented Indian women as hapless, helpless and timid. They were portrayed as uneducated, abused and unable to speak for themselves. This was not the reality of Princess Sophia nor of the Indian women with whom she mixed. These were wealthy women, lawyers, medics, social reformers, educated, emancipated, independent women able to speak for themselves and manage their own affairs; by their behaviour, they challenged the accepted views of the day.

The Women's Freedom League, another suffrage organisation of which Princess Sophia was a member, appears to have had the most personal interaction with Indian women in Britain. In March 1910, *The Vote* reported that "Indian women in this country are showing their sympathy with the suffrage cause; some have become members of the Women's Freedom League so that they may evidence it in a practical way."[19] Mrs. P.L.Roy, Mrs. Bhola Nanth, and Mrs. Mukerjea were all active, articulate, married women not confined to their husbands' pockets. Princess Sophia was an independent woman. Together they empowered women in England and India. Mrs. Roy was president of the London Indian Union Society in 1908 and Mrs. Mukerjea in 1911.[20]

Indian women took part in the Women's Coronation Procession of 1911. This procession, organised by the WSPU, was designed to publicise women's campaign for the right to vote throughout the empire. The Indian women in the procession made a strong visual impact, marching beneath their elephant banner. They sent out a strong statement about the demand for women's rights worldwide. In 1922, six years before Britain granted universal suffrage, some women in India won the right to vote.

Princess Sophia took a great interest in India's political situation; her links with her countrymen were strong. Indian political activity in England centred largely on the student population. It is estimated that in 1910 there were more than seven hundred Indian students in Britain, mostly studying medicine and law, including such famous names as Gandhi, Jinnah and Nehru. The public found Indian students fascinating, exotic and colourful; officials saw them as presenting a moral and political problem. The tone of the special committee of enquiry into Indian students, set up in 1903, showed all the fears and stereotyping of racial prejudice.[21] It was felt that they would succumb to the temptations of city life, be a magnet for white women, satisfy their huge sexual appetites as they pleased, and indulge in drink and fast living. Evidence showed that the vast majority led sober and studious lives. They presented no threat to the modesty and purity of white women. The authorities, however, preferred the more lurid descriptions and used them to justify their close supervision and spying.

The National India Association organised social gatherings where Indian students and interested whites could meet. Princess Sophia attended some of these gatherings. She was present at the India Association 'At Home' held on 1 July 1909, when Curzon Wyllie, ADC to Secretary of State Viscount Morley, was assassinated by Madan Lal Dhingra.[22] After this the India Office increased its monitoring activities of Indians in Britain, and this included the activities of Princess Sophia.

During the First World War she showed her concern and involvement with India by organising patriotic flag days for Punjabi troops in the Indian Army and visiting wounded Indian soldiers at Brighton Pavilion. In 1916 she handed out signed photos of herself to wounded soldiers at Milford-on-Sea.[23] In 1937, she had meetings with Mohan Singh, a member of the Council of the Secretary of State for India.

Princess Sophia's relations with the India Office were not cordial. They were characterised by sharp exchanges and mutual dislike and distrust. Her diary, begun 5 November 1906, has wonderful examples of her spirited correspondence with colonial officials regarding her visits to India. For example, her letter to Sir Charles Rioaz of the India Office: "I wrote to you on Saturday and cannot understand why I have not yet received an answer. Will you kindly let me have an answer this evening as to where I am to stay. I am very sorry that in my haste I did not sign my letter to you but in spite of that I should have thought it was obvious from whom it came!"[24]

She wrote a further indignant letter about her treatment at the British Residency: "Princess Sophia Duleep Singh presents her compliments to the Resident and writes to say if she is being accorded such courtesies as are accorded to travellers of position, she is much surprised as she has been here since the evening of the 7th and so far has seen no-one!"[25]

Lord Morley replied with a long letter blaming lack of information regarding her trip as the reason for her poor reception. He extended an invitation for tea at the Residency. Princess Sophia sent a sharp riposte: "Princess Sophia has no intention of submitting to these vagaries of etiquette or she would not have taken the trouble to write to the India Office before she left England."[26]

The reception at the Residency was not a success! It resulted in another indignant response from Sophia: "The Princess Sophia Duleep Singh was sent into supper on the arm of an unknown and not accorded the courtesies due to her position and royal status."[27]

In contrast, Princess Sophia's welcome from the Indian people could not have been warmer. People flocked to see the granddaughter of the last Maharaja of the Punjab, flowers were strewn at her feet, bands struck up and people mobbed her carriage. The authorities were less than enthusiastic, fearing that she would become a rallying point for dissidents. Police dispersed the crowd. Her visit to Lahore was cut short.

The British government was happier for her to be a princess in England, with all the attention befitting her status, than they were for her to be a princess in India. Princess Sophia wrote to her cousin regarding his young son: "of course you realise that having anything to do with us will not gain him any high posts in India, in fact it will probably do the opposite as the government is not fond of us."[28] Her comments and correspondence show a very real understanding of her position *vis a vis* the British authorities.

Conclusion

By her actions, Princess Sophia made a significant contribution to women's history and specifically to the fight for female emancipation. Her steadfast allegiance, proud defiance and willingness to jeopardise her own position and well-being in support of the suffragettes' cause, earned her notoriety in her own time. History has failed to honour that contribution.

Princess Sophia was an intelligent and resourceful woman well-versed in the political niceties and realities of the day. In contrast to her father who had grandiose schemes for the restoration of his inheritance, Sophia, whilst claiming the recognition due to her royal status, took a much more pragmatic view and instead concentrated her considerable energies on improving the lot of women in her adopted country, England. Women today continue to benefit from her actions.

She was undeniably both princess and activist. She lived the life of an English aristocratic lady whilst retaining strong connections and loyalty to India and to her Sikh heritage. She died in 1948 aged 72. An Indian princess to the end, Princess Sophia requested that her ashes be taken back to India for burial.

disciplines. All of these are useful in establishing the historical and social development of Muslim communities, which add insight into how Muslim communities have come about in Britain.

Since the beginning of Islam, awareness of Muslims in Europe has been negatively tainted. During the history of Western European contact with Muslims it has been in their interests to depict Islam in the worst possible way, primarily to stop conversions to Islam and to alert them to the threat of Muslims to their borders. Although there has been a relative degree of learning and understanding on the part of the British, ignorance and demonisation have led to violence. Muslims have been characterised as barbaric, maddened terrorists or intolerant religious zealots.[2] As much as present day Islamophobia relies on history to provide the substance of its stereotypes, the fear of Muslims today has its own distinctive features, connecting it more to the recent experiences of colonialism, decolonisation, immigration and racism.

Greaves produced a monograph concentrating on the national 'sectarian' influences present within the Muslim communities in Britain. His work pays attention to how these theological and ideological groups impact on communities both locally and internationally. The study however concentrates mainly on British Muslims of South Asian descent and he omits the actions of Arab, African and Turkish Muslim migrants.[3] Many studies have failed to consider the understanding of religious dynamics and paradigms that often shapes the Muslim communities, focusing instead on the cultures and customs that the settlers bring. The cultures and customs which they carry with them are in a way exclusive to their ethnic group and this misleadingly defines the Muslim communities. Few studies exist that explore the religious identity of the various migrant communities and how this plays out in their new environment.[4]

The earlier studies of Muslim communities in Britain printed in the middle to late nineteenth century are regrettably incomplete accounts of their emergence, settlement and ethnography. Arnold makes one of the few rare references to the British Shaykh al-Islam, Abdullah Henry William Quilliam. Arnold indicates his conversion to Islam whilst travelling in Morocco in 1884, noting that Quilliam was impressed by the temperance and good morals of the Muslims. He also documents how Quilliam returned to his native city of Liverpool to set up the Muslim 'Mission'. This brief mention by Arnold is a glimpse into one of the first Muslim communities in Britain, Liverpool.

Pool also makes note of the British Muslim community in Liverpool[5] and its charismatic leader Quilliam. However, Pool dismisses Islam comparing it with Christianity, as he expresses his hope that Christianity is "the true religion of the Western World".[6] Pool's view was the common attitude in the nineteenth century of an unwillingness to accept earlier Muslim communities. Manchester at the close of the nineteenth century had a thriving Muslim community comprising of Syrian, Moroccan, Lebanese and Egyptian Arabs, many of whom were wealthy cotton traders. This early British Muslim community dates back to the 1830s.

The achievements and dynamics of the Liverpool Muslims, their masjid, educational centre, weekly and monthly periodicals, printing and publishing house and the orphanage, the Medina Children's Home, surpass most British Muslim communities active in Britain today. From what has been written on Muslim communities almost none, with the exceptions of Ansari's book and of Lawless' work, are historical studies and even this latter study is only dedicated to a particular period of the early twentieth century.[7]

Antipathy between Islam and the West

Orientalist discourse describes Islam as a large worldwide force that has had a unilinear, antagonistic affiliation with the West throughout history. This essentialist view of history allows the hostile relationship between Islam and the West to be maintained. This view then becomes a rationale for justifying negative perceptions of Islam and of the Muslims that comprise it. Huntington's "clash of civilisations" theory is a modern example of how Islam is considered to be a military, demographic and socio-religious danger.[8] Many, however, reject an overarching truth about the relationship between the West and Islam. Halliday proposes in his hypothesis on "the myth of confrontation" that the ideas in circulation today have their roots in contemporary needs and forces and are sustained on both sides for political purposes.[9] Esposito adds that "Early encounters and confrontations, theological and political, provide the images and folklore which sustain mutual stereotypes, images and suspicions that continue to fuel fears and biases and perpetuate a vision of Islam against the West, of the West against Islam."[10]

Historically, the first encounter between the West and Islam was based on religious scrutiny from the West. Turner suggests that the clash of religions led to global theories of Otherness, the Other constructed to be inferior and incorrect.[11] Daniel illustrates how medieval Christian texts contained identification with Islam is increasing as a deeper understanding can be obtained and as a reaction to racist hostility.[34]

Muslims who came to Britain in the nineteenth and twentieth formed a highly differentiated population in terms of class and ethnicity. Subsequently survival strategies depended on the attitudes taken by the majority white population who viewed them as 'outsiders'. Muslim groups came to Britain at a time when the British Empire and British society was at its zenith. With the Empire at its peak, colonial subjects were viewed as inferiors who deserved to be treated unequally. This subordination translated into poor housing, poor jobs and low levels of income. The exclusion of Muslims did not go uncontested and a degree of acceptance occurred in some localities and at times of national emergencies, such as the two World Wars. Ultimately, at such times it was not the colour of their skins nor their religion that was crucial. Unfortunately, the same cannot be said today: religion has clearly become the main determining factor in identifying who Muslims are.[35]

Conclusion

Today Islamophobia still looms large, noticeably in the aftermath of 9/11 and 7/7. The reaction and depiction of Islam in the media, and the current military occupation of Muslim lands, have strongly reinforced historical prejudices. Muslims have been viewed as the enemy both in literature and in military campaigns throughout history, from the Crusades to Afghanistan. There has remained a current of exaggeration about Islam's backwardness and a major omission of its benefits. One only needs to examine the Liverpool Muslim community to see the good Islam can achieve. The reaction to Western imperialism by Muslims is to return to their religion, a unifying force from a divine source. Also Islam is undoubtedly, for many British Muslims, an identity card in what is essentially a foreign country where they live in cultural concentration and isolation. Attitudes have changed and great strides have been made to integrate Muslims into Britain, but the question still remains: how fully can Islam be integrated into British life? The issue of concern here is that historical patterns have re-emerged and are now becoming even more complex and intricate as British Muslims give birth to the fourth generation.

1. Runnymede Trust, *Islamophobia: a Challenge for Us All* (London: Runnymede Trust, 1997)

2. J. Esposito, *The Islamic Threat: Myth or Reality?* (Oxford: Oxford University Press, 1992).

3. R. Greaves, *Sectarian Influences within Islam in Britain* (Leeds: University of Leeds, 1996).

4. S. Seddon, D. Hussain and N. Malik, *British Muslims Between Assimilation and Segregation* (Markfield: The Islamic Foundation, 2004), p. 2.

5. T. Arnold, *The Preaching of Islam* (Lahore: Muhammad Ashraf, 1892).

6. J. Pool, *Studies in Mohammedanism* (London: Archibald Constable, 1892), p. 402.

7. Seddon, p. 6.

8. S. Huntingdon, *The Clash of Civilisations and the Re-Making of the World Order* (New York: Simon and Schuster, 1996).

9. F. Halliday, *Islam and the Myth of Confrontation* (London: I.B. Tauris, 1996).

10. Esposito, p. 24.

11. B. Turner, 'From Orientalism to Global Sociology', *Sociology*, 23(4), (1989).

12. N. Daniel, *Islam and the West (Oxford: One World*, 1993).

13. G. Munoz, 'Islam's Women Under Western Eyes', at **www.opendemocracy.net/article.498** (accessed 27 March 2009), p. 2.

14. P. Kappert, 'From Romanticism to Colonial Dominance: Historical Changes in the European perception of the Middle East' in J. Hippler and A. Lueg (eds.), *The next Threat: Western Perceptions of Islam* (London: Pluto Press, 1995), 35.

15. T. Abbas, *Muslim Britain* (London: Zed Books, 2005), p. 6.

16. E. Said, *Orientalism* (New York: Vintage, 1978), p. 222.

17. B. Sayyid, *A Fundamental Fear* (London: Zed Books, 1997), p. 17.

18. M. Rodinson, *Marxism and the Muslim World* (London: Zed Press, 1979).

19. Sayyid, p. 120.

20. B. Lewis in Z. Lockman, *Contending Visions of the Middle East* (Cambridge: Cambridge University Press, 2002), p. 216.

21. J. Hippler amd A. Lueg, *The Next Threat* (London: Pluto Press, 1995).

22. F. Halliday, *Islam and the Myth of Confrontation* (London: I.B. Tauris, 1996).

23. Halliday (1996), p.3.

24. M. Anwar, 'Muslims in Britain: 1991 census and other statistical sources', *CSIS Papers Europe 9* (Birmingham: University of Birmingham, 1993); 2001 Census.

25. E. Poole, *Reporting Islam* (London: I.B. Tauris, 2002), p. 19.

26. A. Ahmed and H. Donnan, *Islam, Globalisation and Modernity* (London: Routledge, 2004)

27. Cantle Report, *Community Cohesion* (London: Home Office, 2001).

28. Abbas, pp. 12-13.

29. Islamic Human Rights Commission, *The Oldham Riots: discrimination, deprivation and communal tension in the United Kingdom*, (London: IHRC, 2001), p. 12.

30. Ansari, p.393.

31. Daniel, p. 11.

32. F. Halliday, 'Orientalism and its Critics' in *Islam and the Myth of Confrontation* (London: I.B. Tauris, 1995), p. 160.

33. Ansari, p. 396.

34. Abbasi, p. 13.

35. Ansari, p. 92.

Bibliography

Abbas, T., *Muslim Britain Communities under Pressure*
(London: Zed Books, 2005)

Ahmed, A.S. and Donnan, H., *Islam, Globalisation and Modernity*
(London: Routledge, 2004)

Ansari, H., *'The Infidel Within'. Muslims in Britain since 1800*
(London Hurst, 2004)

Arnold, T.W., *The Preaching of Islam: A History of the Propagation of the
Muslim Faith* (Lahore: Sh. Muhammad Ashraf, 1896)

Daniel, N., *Islam and the West: The Making of an Image*
(Oxford: One World, 1993)

Esposito, J.L., *The Islamic Threat: Myth or Reality?* (Oxford: OUP, 1992)

Greaves, R., *Sectarian Influences within Islam in Britain: with reference to the
concept of 'Ummah' and 'community'* (Leeds: University of Leeds, 1996)

Halliday, F., *Islam and the Myth of Confrontation: Religion and Politics in the
Middle East* (London: I.B. Tauris, 1995)

Halliday, F., *Islam and the Myth of Confrontation: Religion and Politics in the
Middle East* (London: I.B. Tauris, 1996)

Hippler, J. and Lueg, A., *The Next Threat: Western Perceptions of Islam*
(London: Pluto Press, 1995)

Huntington, S., *The Clash of Civilisations and the Remaking of the World
Order* (New York: Simon and Schuster, 1996)

Kappert, P.,'From Romanticism to Colonial Dominance: Historical Changes
in the European Perception of the Middle East' in J. Hippler and A. Lueg
(eds.), *The Next Threat: Western Perceptions of Islam*
(London: Pluto Press, 1995)

Lewis, B. in Lockman, Z., Contending Visions of the Middle East
(Cambridge: Cambridge University Press, 2002)

Pool, J.J., *Studies in Mohammedanism: Historical and Doctrinal,*
(London: Archibald Constable, 1892)

Poole, E., *Reporting Islam: Media Representations of British Muslims,*
(London: I.B. Tauris, 2002)

Rodinson, M., *Marxism and the Muslim World* (London: Zed Press, 1979)

Said, E., *Orientalism* (New York: Vintage, 1978)

Sayyid, B.S., *A Fundamental Fear: Eurocentrism and the Emergence of Islam*
(London: Zed Books, 1997)

Seddon, S., Hussain, D. and Malik, N., *British Muslims between Assimilation and Segregation: Historical, Legal and Social Realities* (Markfield: The Islamic Foundation, 2004)

Journal articles

Halliday, F., 'The Millet of Manchester: Arab Merchants and Cotton Trade', *British Journal of Middle Eastern Studies*, BRISMES, 19 (2) (1993)

Turner, B.S., 'From Orientalism to Global Sociology', *Sociology*, 23 (4) (1989)

Articles, Papers and Reports

Anwar, M., 'Muslims in Britain: 1991 census and other statistical sources', *CSIC Papers Europe 9* (Birmingham: University of Birmingham, 1993)

Cantle Report, *Community Cohesion: a Report of the Independent Review Team* (London: Home Office, 2001)

Islamic Human Rights Commission, *The Oldham Riots: discrimination, deprivation and communal tension in the United Kingdom*, (London: IHRC, 2001)

Runnymede Trust, *Islamophobia: a Challenge for Us All* (London: Runnymede Trust, 1997)

Websites

BBC website,
http://www.bbc.co.uk/religion/religions/islam/beliefs/jihad_2.shtml
(accessed 5 February 2009)

Munoz, G., 'Islam's women under Western eyes',
www.opendemocracy.net/article.498 (accessed 27 March 2009)